CW00647659

THE MAGICAL CALENDAR

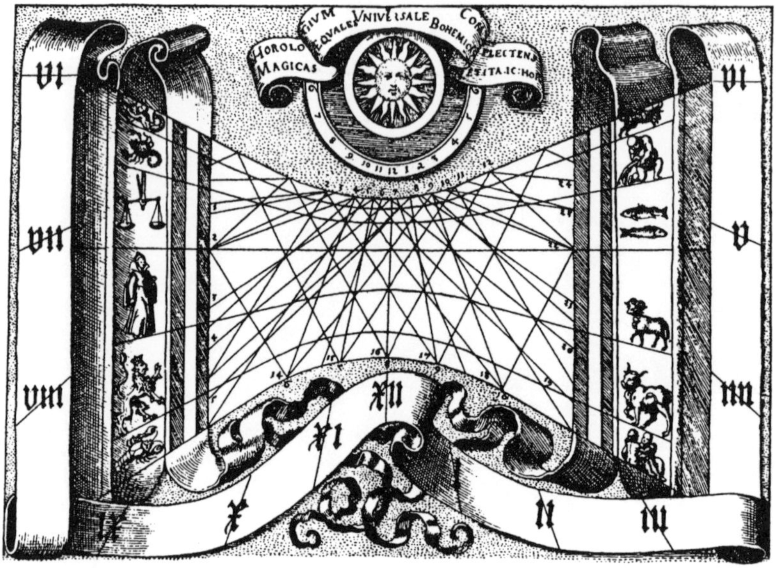
HOROLO
MAGICAS
VNIVERSALE
BOHEMIC
PLECTENS
VI
VII
VIII
IX
X
XI
XII
II
III
IIII
V
VI

THE MAGICAL CALENDAR

A Synthesis of Magical Symbolism from the Seventeenth-Century Renaissance of Medieval Occultism

Translation and Commentary
by Adam McLean

Magnum Opus Hermetic Sourceworks #1

Phanes Press
1994

This work, part of the Magnum Opus Hermetic Sourceworks series, was previously published in a handbound edition, limited to 250 copies, in 1979. The Magnum Opus Hermetic Sourceworks series is published under the General Editorship of Adam McLean. This new edition has been revised and reset by Phanes Press and is issued with a 18 x 36 inch poster-size reproduction of the original Magical Calendar engraving from 1620.

© 1994 by Adam McLean.

All rights reserved. No part of this publication may be reproduced or transmitted in any form, with the exception of short excerpts used in reviews, without the permission in writing from the publisher.

98 97 96 95 94   5 4 3 2 1

Published by Phanes Press, PO Box 6114, Grand Rapids, MI 49516, USA.

Library of Congress Cataloging-in-Publication Data

Calendarium naturale magicum. English and latin.
The Magical calendar : a synthesis of magical symbolism from the seventeenth century Renaissance of Medieval occultism / translated and edited by Adam McLean.
p.   cm.
Parallel Latin text and English translation.
Originally published: Edinburgh : Magnum Opus Hermetic Sourceworks, 1979. (Magnum Opus Hermetic Sourceworks ; #1)
Includes bibliographical references.
ISBN 0-933999-32-1 (alk. paper) : $32.00. — ISBN 0-933999-33-X (pbk. : alk. paper) : $18.00
1. Magic—Early works to 1800.   I. McLean, Adam.   II. Title.
III. Series: Magnum Opus Hermetic Sourceworks (Series) : no. 1.
BF1601.C3413   1993
133—dc20   93-34766
CIP

This book is printed on alkaline paper which conforms to the permanent paper standard developed by the National Information Standards Organization.

Printed and bound in the United States

Contents

Introduction

The *Magical Calendar* is one of the largest single copperplate engravings ever made. Measuring 48 by 24 inches, it was published at Frankfurt in 1620 during the early seventeenth-century renaissance of Hermetic publishing.

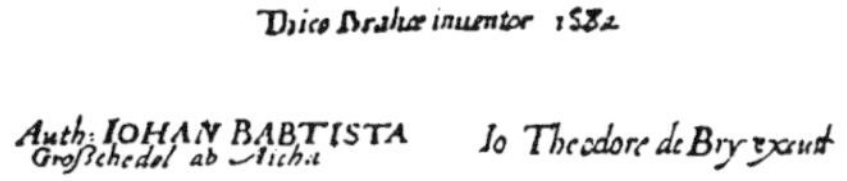
Tÿico Brahæ inuentor 1582
Auth: IOHAN BABTISTA
Großchedel ab Aicha
Io Theodore de Bry excud

The original engraving of the *Magical Calendar* bears three names at the bottom right corner. These were erased on the 1922 de Mély reprint which Phanes Press used for the poster illustration which accompanies this book.

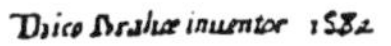

Although his name appears at the bottom right hand corner of the plate, the *Magical Calendar* probably has no direct connection with Tycho Brahe (1541–1601), the famous Danish astronomer and astrologer, whose precise observations of the movements of the planets enabled Kepler to construct his laws of planetary motion. It seems most likely that the well known name of Tycho Brahe was associated with the *Magical Calendar* in order to gain a degree of publicity and supposed authority for the work. Certainly there is nothing in Brahe's accepted corpus of writings of a similar nature. Indeed the astronomical and astrological content of the plate is minimal: there are but three tables of purely astronomical import. The *Calendar* is a vehicle for a synthesis of magical and numerical symbolic philosophy, and there are no internal references which would otherwise connect the work with Tycho Brahe. The 1582 date is obviously spurious.

Auth: IOHAN BABTISTA
Großchedel ab Aicha

It is perhaps more significant that the name of Johann Baptista Grosschedel von Aicha appears as author on the left hand side of the plate. Almost nothing is known of Grosschedel except that he wrote two books on Hermetic alchemical matters, the *Proteus Mercurialis Geminus*, and the *Trifolium Hermeticum*, both published at the same place as the *Magical Calendar*, i.e. at Frankfurt in 1629. It seems likely that Grosschedel was the editor and compiler of the correspondences and symbolism, though later editors of this material have sought to obscure and undervalue his contribution. In the British Library there is a manuscript MS. Harley 3420, in Latin with some short sections in German, which is obviously important for an assessment of Grosschedel.

On the recto of folio 1 is the title:

> Dispositio Numerorum Magica Ab Unitate usque ad Duodenarium Collecta, singulari industria, compilatione diversa, magno labore, et investigatione sibi suisque. A Joanne Baptista Grosschedelio Equite Romano ab Aicha, Philomago, Lucisque a Gratiae, a Naturae [indagatori] Vigilantissimo. Anno 1614.

The verso reads:

> H. C. A. Lib 2. C. 3. . . . Descriptio Calendarii Magici Naturalis perpetuus Occultae seu secretioris Philosophiae cognitionem et contemplationem complectens. . . . NB . . . Calendarium . . . Martin Ludwig von Remchingen [?] . . . durch Theodoricum de Bry . . . Anno 1619.
> ["H.C.A. Lib 2. C." is a reference to Henry Cornelius Agrippa, Occult Philosophy, Book 2, Chapter 3.]

This manuscript could well be the archetype from which the

Calandarium was constructed. All the information on the *Magical Calendar* is included in this manuscript along with extra material that does not appear on the engraving. However, a number of later dates in the 1630s also appear in the margins, so one cannot be sure without further study whether this manuscript predates the printed version or is a later copy.

Io Theodore de Bry excud

The last important figure to be associated with the *Magical Calendar* is Johannes Theodorus de Bry (1561–1623). He was the eldest son of Dirk Theodorus de Bry, a skillful producer of prints and illustrated books, who established the family printing business in Frankfurt on Maine around 1590. Johann surpassed his father both in technical skill and in composition, and he began to specialize in the publication of emblem books, alchemical and mystical writings, in particular the important encyclopedic surveys by Robert Fludd of Hermetic philosophy and some of the works of the Rosicrucian writer Michael Maier. The copperplate engravings produced by his press are unsurpassed in technical brilliance, but in addition to this de Bry and the fellow engravers in his company possessed the rare ability to express philosophical and spiritual ideas in pictorial form.

Little is known of the background of de Bry but it has been suggested that he and his family were members of an esoteric sect known as the Family of Love, which developed certain mystical and allegorical interpretations of biblical texts. The Family of Love sect seems to have had a considerable involvement in the world of publishing during the early seventeenth century, and may have been instrumental in publishing some of Giordano Bruno's work and reprinting John Dee's *Hieroglyphic Monad*. Whatever may be made of de Bry's involvement in esoteric groups, he certainly played a vital part in the promulgation of that stream of wisdom which came to the surface in the early seventeenth century as Rosicrucianism. According to both Ferguson in *Bibliotheca Chemica* and the British Library catalogue, the engraver of the

Magical Calendar was Mathieu Merian, de Bry's son in law, a prolific artist who was responsible for the complex series of engravings in the works of J. D. Mylius, the series of fifty emblematic figures in Michael Maier's *Atalanta Fugiens*, and many other titles. Indeed, he provided illustrations for most of the important Hermetic books of this period.

Sources

It is possible to identify some of the original sources from which the *Magical Calendar* was compiled. The most important primary source is Henry Cornelius Agrippa's *De occulta philosophia libri tres*, first published at Cologne in 1533, but which went through many editions in the 16th century. Agrippa uses the same format—tables of correspondences connected with the numbers one to twelve—but, although there are similarities in the two lists, the *Magical Calendar* is by no means a straight copy of Agrippa's tables. Much material is added, and some deleted. Interestingly, while Agrippa provides in the lowest section of each table a demonic correspondence in the infernal world, the *Magical Calendar* engraving does not include these. It would seem that the compiler wished not to include any "demonic" or "evil" associations, and thus desired to present the *Calendarium* as an example of the purest, spiritual, white magic. Other items which have been borrowed from Agrippa are the magic squares, the Intelligences and Spirits of the seven planets, together with their sigils and seals.

Another obvious source is the *Heptameron* or "Magical Elements" of Peter of Abano (1250–1318), which provides us with the seven Archangelic sigils, the four names of the Earth and the Angels of the four seasons. The "Archidoxes of Magic," a work pseudonymously ascribed to Paracelsus (1493–1541) furnishes a series of sigils for the twelve signs, and the table of the transmutation of the metals. The compiler of the *Magical Calendar* also possibly had access to some examples of magical manuscripts circulating in the early seventeenth century, a number of which had lists of correspondences and angel names.

Later Printed Editions of the *Calendarium*

In the late eighteenth century du Chenteau published a large engraving, the *Calendrier Magique et Perpétuel*, which was derived from the seventeenth-century engraving, but with many additions. The correspondences had been translated into French, and were now joined by diagrams copied from Georg von Welling's *Opus Mago Cabbalisticum* (1719), Robert Fludd's *Utriusque cosmi historia* (1617–21), and a number of engravings from seventeenth century alchemical works. The engraving was also given a masonic dimension by placing the two pillars of Jakin and Boteaz (sic) on the top left and right. The full title of this version is:

> *Calendrier magique et perpétuel contenant la contemplation des choses les plus profondes, et les plus secrettes, avec la connoissance complette de la philosophie. Le Tout Deffiné et Gravé dans un nouvel Ordre, Rectifié et Combiné, avec les Articles du Titre suivant. Par le T. V. F. du Chenteau Mathematicien. . . . Carte philosophique et mathématique dédiée à son A.R. Monseigneur le Duc Charles Alexandre de Lorraine et de Bar. . .* Bruxelles, 1755.

The du Chenteau engraving was reissued by Giuseppe Wopaletzky at Turin in 1866, under the title *Teletes* (reprinted Milan: Archè, 1977).

The correspondences of the *Magical Calendar* were also shown in a book by Fortunatus de Grippis, *De superstitione et vinculis daemonum secundum Aegyptiorum et Chaldaeorum dogmata iuxta etiam Tychonis Calendarium accurate emendatum*, Milan, 1805.

In 1922 F. de Mély edited and published at Paris a facsimile reprint of the *Virga Aurea*, "the heavenly golden rod of the Blessed Virgin in seventy two praises." The "rod" refers to the letters of a language. This large engraving (about 20 by 32 inches) was originally published in 1616 at Rome, and was the work of James Bonaventure Hepburn (1573–1620), a Scot who was the Keeper of Oriental Books and Manuscripts at the Vatican library during the early part of the seventeenth century. Hepburn, a most respected linguist and scholar, seems to have had a considerable interest in the occult, and it is remarkable that he was able to publish his translation from Hebrew into Latin of a kabbalistic text entitled "the Kettar Malcuth of Rabbi Solomon." He must have achieved high standing and reputation to be able to do this quite openly, during a period in the history of the Roman Church when heresy and occultism were proscribed. Witness how the Church dealt at this time with both Galileo and Giordano Bruno.

The *Virga Aurea* plate consists of a list of seventy two alphabets, including both the letters of living languages and also a large number of artificial magical alphabets, the letters of which are also sigils. These lists are headed by a large image of the Virgin.

De Mély in his 1922 edition includes the *Magical Calendar*, printed full size but split into three separate plates, as if it were part of the *Virga Aurea*, when it is obvious even from a superficial consideration of the engraving styles that they are not part of the same work. It seems most likely that these two large engravings, being from the same period and bearing strange magical signs, were bound together by a previous owner or librarian, and de Mély assumed that they were all one work.

Some Manuscript Copies of the *Calendarium*

I have already referred to the British Library MS. Harley 3420. This is probably the earliest manuscript. At the time of writing this introduction, I have not been able to determine whether it predates the publication of the *Magical Calendar*. Much could be gained by a detailed analysis of this manuscript.

Another important seventeenth-century manuscript is in the National Library of Austria in Vienna, MS. Lat. 11313. (A facsimile is shown in K. A. Nowotny's edition of Agrippa's *Occulta philosophia*, published at Graz in 1967.) This beautifully drawn manuscript attempts to pass itself off as being much earlier by bearing the date "1503," and presents itself as if emanated from the circle of Johannes Trithemius (1462–1516), the Abbot of Sponheim, a profound scholar of the magical and Hermetic traditions. Trithemius was able to gather at his monastery an extensive library of manuscripts, and as his reputation as a scholar of this arcane material grew, he gathered a small group of pupils whom he inspired to work with this store of Hermetic lore. He was particularly influential upon the two most important Hermetic writers of the sixteenth century, Henry Cornelius Agrippa von Nettesheim (1486–1535), and Philippus Theophrastus Paracelsus (1493–1541). The Vienna manuscript contains on folio 2 this attempted link with Trithemius:

> You who aspire to search for the greatness of the natural magic of Johannes Trithemius, Abbot of Sponheim, should be a good and pious man, honourable and constant in word and deed, of firm faith in God, wise, and greedy for nothing except our wisdom. In the year of the Lord, 1503.

The manuscript, however, betrays itself as being copied from the printed plate, as the copyist has misread a slip of the engraver's tool under the letter "R" in the word "BARCHIEL" which makes it appear like a "B," and the Vienna MS. transcribes this word in lower case as "Babchiel." The "1503" date is also entirely fictitious as the manuscript includes the astronomical table with references to new and old style dates, which was brought about by the revision of the calendar by Pope Gregory in 1582. The copyist of this manuscript was attempting in a rather clumsy way to suggest that the *Magical Calendar* arose from the work of Trithemius. In a way, perhaps he was correct. The *Calendarium* draws heavily from Agrippa, and it may well be that he in turn gained much of his knowledge of this elaborate magical symbolism from his period under the tutelage of Trithemius. However, more primary research would be needed into the manuscripts and associations of Trithemius in order to sustain this thesis.

An early eighteenth-century Italian manuscript of the *Magical Calendar* in the Bibliotheca Philosophica Hermetica in Amsterdam also suggests this link with Trithemius. This manuscript is the *Operatio astronomica* of Rutilio Benincasa and is dated 1708. On page 92 we find the note "Notizie kabalistiche sul Kalendario Magico. Questo Kalendario trovato nei Mstti di Rutilio Benincasa . . . e quella chiave misteriosa ed occulta che tanto lodo l'abbate

Tritemio, Cornelio Agrippa . . . Non è altro proprio questo che una riunione di tutti gli scritti misteriosi de questi autori." Thus this note suggests that the *Magical Calendar* in the hand of Rutilio Benincase (which begins on page 97 of the manuscript), is nothing other than a compilation from the writings and documents of Trithemius and Agrippa.

One of the most beautifully illustrated of the later manuscript copies of the Calendarium is in Yale University, Mellon collection, MS. 72, dated around 1700.

There are a number of other later manuscript copies of the *Calendarium* which I will list here; however I do not pretend that this is a complete listing:

London, Wellcome Institute, MS. 321. [c.1650].
Johann Baptist Grosschedel. Annotations sur le Calendrier naturel et cabalistiq[ue].
[By an unnamed commentator. Interleaved is a copy, cut up into eleven strips, of the engraved broadside "Calendarium naturale magicum perpetuum," published by J. T. de Bry.]

London, Wellcome Institute, MS. 2640. [1716]
Grosschedel, Johann Baptist. Calendarium naturale magicum perpetuum profundissimam rerum secretissimarum contemplationem totiusque philosophiae cognitionem completens. Copied by F. Vallée, mathématicien en 1716 à Paris.
[Illustrated with pen and wash drawings.]

London, Wellcome Institute, MS. 2641. [Mid 18th century.]
Grosschedel, Johann Baptist. Calendarium naturale magicum perpetuum profundissimam rerum secretissimarum contemplationem totiusque philosophiae cognitionem completens.
[Illustrated with pen drawings.]
[Armorial bookplate of Ignatius Dominicus S. R. Comes de Chorinsky.]

Glasgow University Library, MS. Ferguson 2. [Early 19th century.]
[Grosschedel ab Aïcha.]
Magnum Grimorium sive Calendarium Naturale Magicum perpetuum

profundissimarum rerum secretissimarum contemplationem totiusque philosophiae cognitionem complectens.
[This is a copy of the "Calendarium Naturale Magicum," compiled by Grosschedel von Aicha and published by de Bry in 1620. The emblematic figures from the original engraving have been cut up into individual sections and pasted into this manuscript, and the text from the original plate added in black and red lettering. Each page is set within a red border decorated at the top. The *Calendarium Naturale Magicum* is thus analyzed in its various sections "Tabula Prima . . . Tabula Duodecima." Additional text material in way of explanation and examples has been added to the sections within the Tabula Septima dealing with the seven planetary onomantic tables of fortune.]
[Note inside back cover]: "This looks like one of Bacstrom's Ms."

Los Angeles, Manly Palmer Hall [P.R.S.], MS. 191. [18th century.]
[Part of Cagliostro Collection, MS. 119.]
Des Nombres. Voicy en qu'en raport le Savant Mitologiste, ou le Adam Mitologue de ce Siecle, Mr. Antoine Joseph Pernety, Religieux Benedictin de St. Maur En 1758. Sur qu'il en a retire de la Sublime carte de tycho-brahe.
[Some of the material is taken from the Magical Calendar engraving.]

Rome, Biblioteca dell'Accademia dei Lincei. MS. Verginelli-Rota 36. [19th century.]
Calendarium Naturale Magicum Perpetuum Profundissimam Rerum Secretissimam Contemplationem, Totiusque Philosophiae Cognitionem Complectens.

Dresden, MS. N. 67a. [18th Century]
Calendarium Naturale Magicum Perpetuum profundissimarum rerum secretissimarum contemplationem totiusque philosophiae cognitionem complectens. Authore [Iohannes Baptiste] Grosschedel ab Aïcha [without figures].

Conclusion

The *Magical Calendar* made its appearance in 1620. It provided a synthesis of the magical symbolism of the Renaissance and medieval periods, arising out of the esoteric school of Johannes Trithemius, and was worked into an organized form suitable for the early seventeenth century by a publisher with Rosicrucian connections. It thus contributed towards the magical symbolism side of the Hermetic revival in the seventeenth century. The *Calendar* continued to inspire Hermeticists, as we can see from the manuscript copies and printed versions, into the present century.

Although it is possible to view the *Magical Calendar* in a merely historical context, it would be quite wrong to see it as something bound in the past. The esoteric content of the *Magical Calendar* is not dead. It can still be pursued today, for the *Magical Calendar* enshrines a way of synthesis that has become more and more lost to humanity since the Renaissance, with the rise and eventual dominance of the abstract, analytical mode of thought. Magical or Hermetic thinking is the ability to see ideas as part of a whole—to see the interconnections, the correspondences, between seemingly diverse events, things and ideas. The magician thinks in terms of the fourfoldness in the world, or finds the sevenfoldness of the planetary archetypes all around him.

We need to reconnect with this Hermetic mode of thought, this magical way of looking at the world. Alchemy and symbolic magic, two facets of Hermeticism, are not weird offshoots of human eccentricity belonging to a now dead phase of our culture, but indeed contain the germ of the future development of our consciousness.

What lives in the Hermetic tradition as spiritual impulse will have to be recovered and transformed through human activity into a philosophy, a path of spiritual training and inner development, that is in harmony with the present stage of the evolution of the human soul. The magical mode of thought enshrined in the *Magical Calendar* will always live within us as a source, an inner treasury, that provides the key to the nature of our being.

During the closing years of the twentieth century, humankind has penetrated even more deeply into the material sphere; in consequence, we now require a spiritual philosophy and esotericism that also encounters the material directly. This is indeed found in Hermeticism, both in alchemy, which works spiritually with substances, and in symbolic magic, which works with colors, geometric forms, smells and sounds to transform the human soul.

The *Magical Calendar* is a bridge between what lived in early seventeenth-century Hermeticism and what can come into being as the future evolution of human consciousness. In this sense it is an important and still living work.

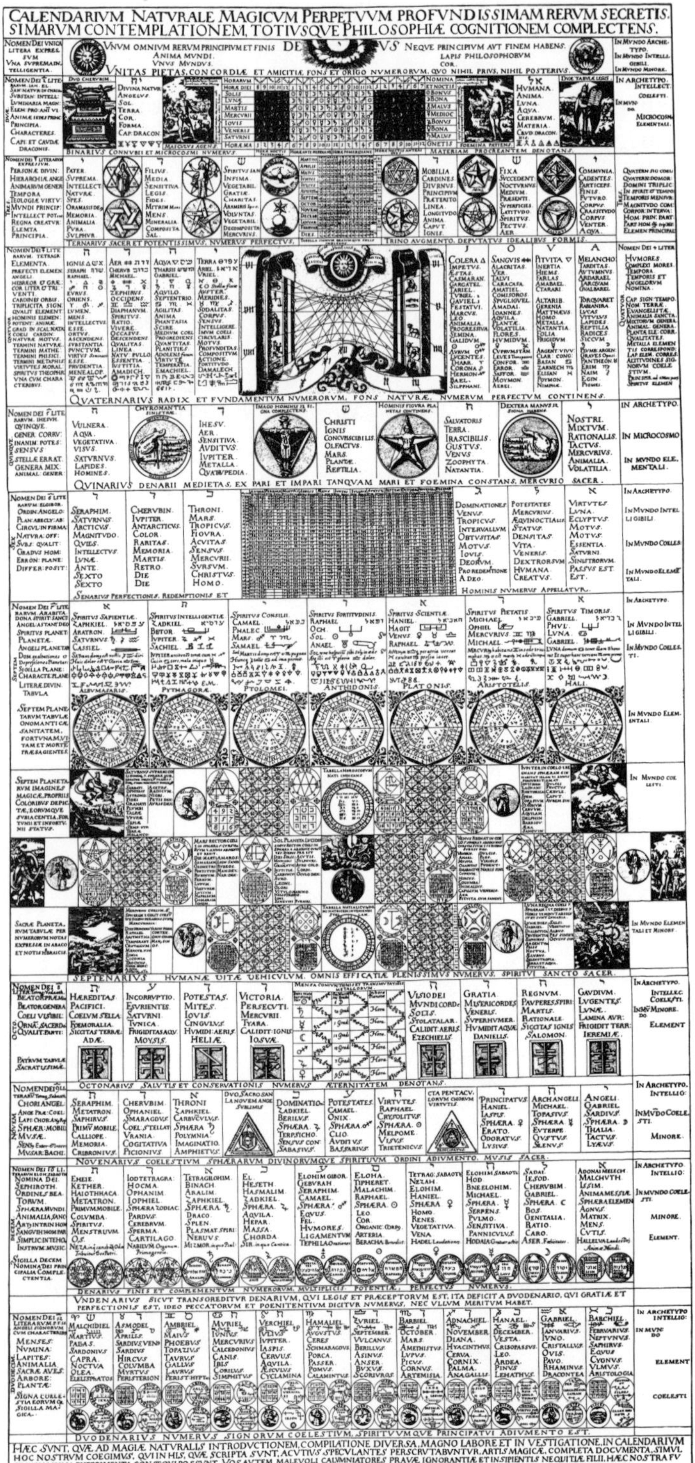
CALENDARIVM NATVRALE MAGICVM PERPETVVM PROFVNDISSIMAM RERVM SECRETISSIMARVM CONTEMPLATIONEM, TOTIVSQVE PHILOSOPHIÆ COGNITIONEM COMPLECTENS.
VNITAS PIETAS, CONCORDIÆ ET AMICITIÆ FONS ET ORIGO NVMERORVM, QVO NIHIL PRIVS, NIHIL POSTERIVS.
QVATERNARIVS RADIX ET FVNDAMENTVM NVMERORVM, FONS NATVRÆ, NVMERVM PERFECTVM CONTINENS.
HÆC SVNT, QVÆ AD MAGIÆ NATVRALIS INTRODVCTIONEM, COMPILATIONE DIVERSA, MAGNO LABORE ET IN VESTIGATIONE, IN CALENDARIVM HOC NOSTRVM COEGIMVS, QVI IN HIS, QVÆ SCRIPTA SVNT, ACVTIVS SPECVLANTES PERSCRVTABVNTVR, ARTIS MAGICÆ, COMPLETA DOCVMENTA, SIMVL ET INFALLIBILIA EXPERIMENTA CONSEQVI POSSVNT. VOS AVTEM MALEVOLI CALVMNIATORES PRAVÆ IGNORANTIÆ ET INSIPIENTIS NEQVITIÆ FILII, HÆC NOSTRA FVGITE ATQVE INTACTA RELINQVITE

The Magical Calendar

DE י VS

VNVS REX STELLARVM FONS LVCIS

VNVS QVOQVE PHOENIX IN MVNDO

ONE

The one lettered Name of God: Yod

י

One, the beginning and end of all things,
without beginning or end.

One Soul of the World

One World

One Philosopher's Stone

One Heart

One Supreme Intelligence

Unity, piety, the source of harmony and friendship and origin of the Numbers, having nothing preceding or following.

One King of the Stars, the Source of Light.

Also, one Phoenix in the World.

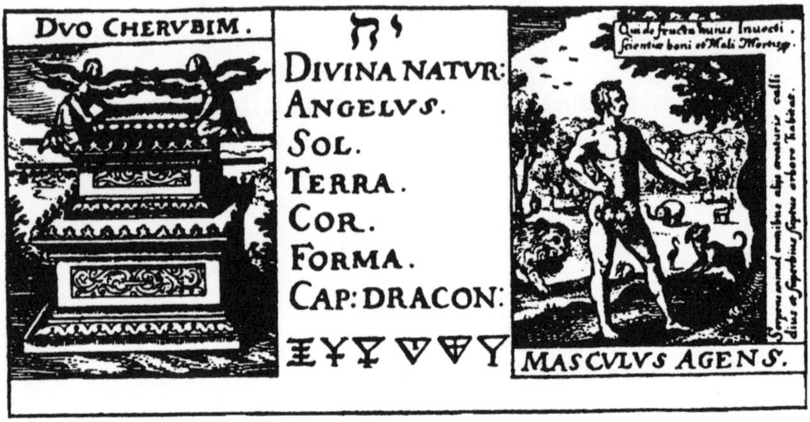
DVO CHERVBIM.
יה
DIVINA NATVR:
ANGELVS.
SOL.
TERRA.
COR.
FORMA.
CAP: DRACON:
MASCVLVS AGENS.

FOEMINA PATIENS.
אל
HVMANA.
ANIMA.
LVNA.
AQVA.
CEREBRVM.
MATERIA.
CAVD: DRACON:
NIS.
DVÆ TABVLÆ LEGIS.

The two lettered Name of God: Iah, El

	יה	אל
Two Sacred Natures in Christ	Divine Nature	Human Nature
Two Substances of Understanding	Angelic	Soul
Two Great Luminaries	Sun	Moon
Two Elements through which the Soul Lives	Earth	Water
Two Seats of the Principles of the Soul	Heart	Brain
Two Principles	Form	Material
Head or Tail of the Dragon	Dragon's Head	Dragon's Tail
Twofold Characters[1]		

Male Active
Death followed from this fruit of the knowledge of Good and Evil.

The serpent, an animal distinguished from all other creatures by godlike cleverness and arrogance, lives beneath the Tree.

Female Passive
She eats of the Tree that she might share an eternal sympathy.

The knowledge of this tree is impressed naturally, through the serpent sitting beneath this tree of Luciferic death.

The Binary—The number of marriage and of the Microcosm, denoting material procreation.

HORARVM	TARAC	SASVR	AGLO	CALER VA	SALA	YAYN	LNOR	NASIA	SALA	SADED ALI	TAMVR	OVRE
HORÆ DIEI	8	9	10	11	12	1	2	3	4	5	6	7
SOLIS	☿	☽	♄	♃	♂	☉	♀	☿	☽	♄	♃	♂
LVNÆ	♃	♂	☉	♀	☿	☽	♄	♃	♂	☉	♀	☿
MARTIS	♀	☿	☽	♄	♃	♂	☉	♀	☿	☽	♄	♃
MERCVRII	♄	♃	♂	☉	♀	☿	☽	♄	♃	♂	☉	♀
IOVIS	☉	♀	☿	☽	♄	♃	♂	☉	♀	☿	☽	♄
VENERIS	☽	♄	♃	♂	☉	♀	☿	☽	♄	♃	♂	☉
SATVRNI	♂	☉	♀	☿	☽	♄	♃	♂	☉	♀	☿	☽
HORÆMA	1	2	3	4	5	6	7	8	9	10	11	12
	HORÆ NOCTIS POSTERIORES					HORÆ ANTE MERIDIANE						

This illustration shows the hours of the Day and Night with their planetary associations, for the seven days of the week. ☉☽♃ *and* ♀ *are seen as being of good influence, while* ♂ *and* ♄ *are of evil aspect, and* ☿ *has both these facets.*

Choosing the correct hour for a magical operation was deemed of major importance in Renaissance magic, and tables with this information are found in many books and manuscripts.

The names of the hours, as seen above, are also found in the Heptameron *of Peter of Abano, though there are minor variations of spelling. These are shown opposite for comparison.*

TWO

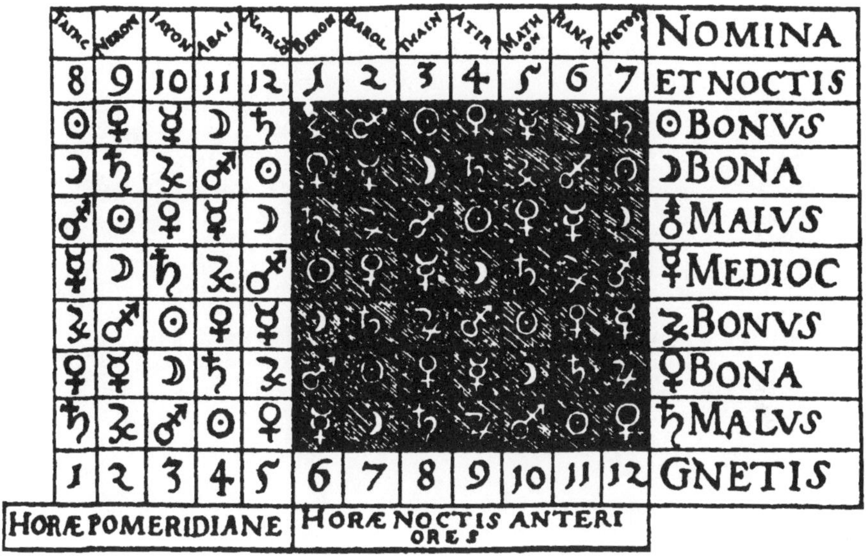
NOMINA
ETNOCTIS
BONVS
BONA
MALVS
MEDIOC
BONVS
BONA
MALVS
GNETIS
HORÆ POMERIDIANE
HORÆ NOCTIS ANTERI ORES

Hours of the Day

	Magical Calendar	Heptameron
1	Yayn	Yayn
2	Lanor	Janor
3	Nasnia	Nasnia
4	Sala	Salla
5	Sadedali	Sadedali
6	Tanur	Thamur
7	Ovre	Ourer
8	Tainc	Tanic
9	Neron	Neron
10	Iayon	Jayon
11	Abai	Abay
12	Natalon	Natalon

Hours of the Night

	Magical Calendar	Heptameron
1	Beron	Beron
2	Barol	Barol
3	Thain	Thanu
4	Atir	Athir
5	Mathon	Maton
6	Rana	Rana
7	Netos	Netos
8	Tarac	Tafrac
9	Sasur	Sassur
10	Aglo	Aglo
11	Caerva	Calerna
12	Salam	Salam

י		ר		ש	
PATER. SVPREMA. INTELLECT: NATVRÆ. SPES. ORAMASIS DE9 MEMORIA. ANIMALIA. PVRA. SVLPHVR.	 	FILIVS. MEDIA. SENSITIVA. LEGIS. FIDES. MITRIM Mens. MENS. MINERALIA. COMPOSITA. SAL.	 	SPIRITVS SAN INFIMA. VEGETABIL: GRATIÆ. CHARITAS. ARAMIRIS Spirit. VOLVNTAS. VEGETABIL: DECOMPOSITA MERCVRIVS.	 

THREE

The three lettered Name of God: Shaddai

	י	ד	ש
Three Divine Persons	Father	Son	Holy Spirit
Three Angelic Hierarchies	Supreme	Middle	Lower
Three Species of Soul	Intellectual	Sentient	Vegetable
Three Rules	Of Nature	Of Law	Of Grace
Three Theological Virtues	Hope	Faith	Charity
Three World Principles	Oramasis God	Mitrim Mind	Aramiris Spirit
Three Intellectual Powers	Memory	Mind	Will
Three Kingdoms of Creation	Animal	Mineral	Vegetable
Three Elements	Pure	Compounded	Decomposed
Three Principles	Sulphur	Salt	Mercury

The Ternary, sacred and most powerful, the perfect number—to add to the Three, departs from the ideal forms.

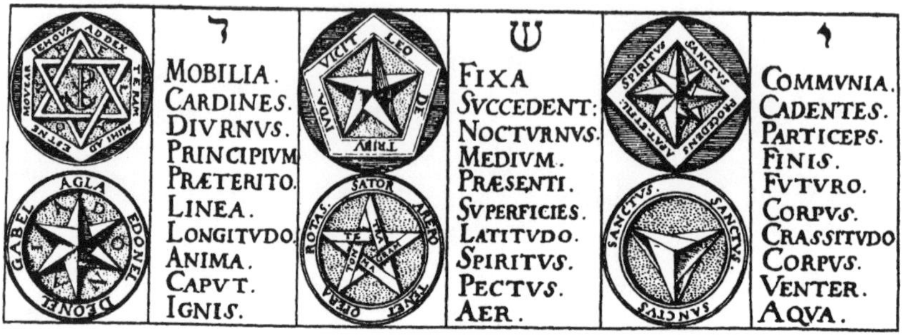
MOBILIA.
CARDINES.
DIVRNVS.
PRINCIPIVM
PRÆTERITO.
LINEA.
LONGITVDO.
ANIMA.
CAPVT.
IGNIS.
FIXA
SVCCEDENT:
NOCTVRNVS.
MEDIVM.
PRÆSENTI.
SVPERFICIES.
LATITVDO.
SPIRITVS.
PECTVS.
AER.
COMMVNIA.
CADENTES.
PARTICEPS.
FINIS.
FVTVRO.
CORPVS.
CRASSITVDO
CORPVS.
VENTER.
AQVA.
AGLA
GABEL
EDONEL
DEONEL
VICIT LEO DE TRIBV IVDA
SATOR AREPO TENET OPERA ROTAS
SPIRITVS SANCTVS
SANCTVS

THREE

	ו	ש	י
Three Quaternities of Celestial Sign	Movable	Fixed	Common
Three Quaternities of Zodiacal House	Angular Cardinal	Succedent Exaltation	Cadent Fall
Three Masters of the Houses	Day	Night	Twilight
Three Spirits in Time	Beginning	Middle	End
Three Measures of Time	Past	Present	Future
Three Measures of Magnitude	Length	Area	Volume
Three Dimensions of a Body	Length	Breadth	Thickness
Three Principal Parts of Man	Soul	Spirit	Body
Three Parts of Man Corresponding to the Three Worlds	Head	Breast	Belly
Three Elementary Principles	Fire	Air	Water

2

THREE

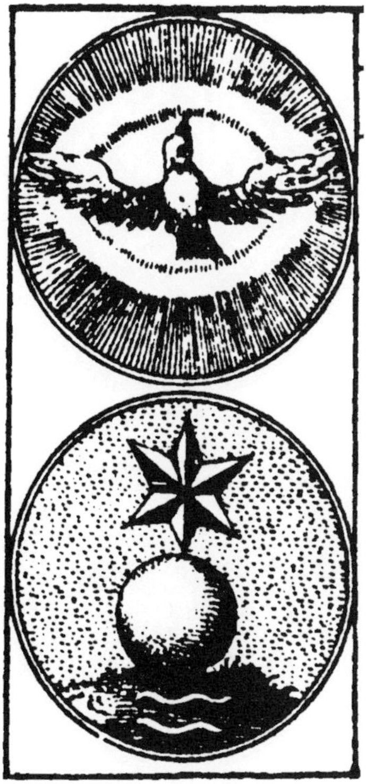

IEHOVA
AD DEX
TERMM
MIHI AD
ESTNE
MOVEAR
AGLA
EDONEL
DEONEL
GABEL
I A D O N A

2

VICIT LEO DE TRIBV IVDA.
SATOR AREPO TENET OPERA ROTAS.
TE TRA GRAM MA TON
SPIRITVS SANCTVS PROCEDENS APAT: ETFIL:
SANCTVS. SANCTVS. SANCTVS.

2

THREE

MARTIVS.	20 / 21	22 / 23	24 / 25	26 / 27	28 / ♈	1 / 2	3 / 4	5 / 6	7 / 8	9 / 10	11 / 12	13 / 14	15 / 16	17 / 18	19 / 20	21	31
APRILIS.	22 / 23	24 / 25	26 / 27	28 / 29	30 / 31	♉ / 1	2 / 3	4 / 5	6 / 7	8 / 9	10 / 11	12 / 13	14 / 15	16 / 17	18 / 19		30
MAIVS	20 / 21	22 / 23	24 / 25	26 / 27	28 / 29	30 / ♊	1 / 2	3 / 4	5 / 6	7 / 8	9 / 10	11 / 12	13 / 14	15 / 16	17 / 18	19	31
IVNIVS.	20 / 21	22 / 23	24 / 25	26 / 27	28 / 29	30 / 31	♋ / 1	2 / 3	4 / 5	6 / 7	8 / 9	10 / 11	12 / 13	14 / 15	16 / 17		30
IVLIVS.	18 / 19	20 / 21	22 / 23	24 / 25	26 / 27	28 / 29	30 / ♌	1 / 2	3 / 4	5 / 6	7 / 8	9 / 10	11 / 12	13 / 14	15 / 16	17	31
AVGVSTvs	18 / 19	20 / 21	22 / 23	24 / 25	26 / 27	28 / 29	30 / 31	♍ / 1	2 / 3	4 / 5	6 / 7	8 / 9	10 / 11	12 / 13	14 / 15	16	31
SEPTEM:	17 / 18	19 / 20	21 / 22	23 / 24	25 / 26	27 / 28	29 / 30	♎	1 / 2	3 / 4	5 / 6	7 / 6	9 / 10	11 / 12	13 / 14		30
OCTOB:	15 / 16	17 / 18	19 / 20	21 / 22	23 / 24	25 / 26	27 / 28	29 / 30	31 ♏ / 1	2 / 3	4 / 5	6 / 7	8 / 9	10 / 11	12 / 13	14	31
NOVEM:	15 / 16	17 / 18	19 / 20	21 / 22	23 / 24	25 / 26	27 / 28	29 / 30	31 / ♐	1 / 2	3 / 4	5 / 6	7 / 8	9 / 10	11 / 12	13 / 14	30
DECEMB:	15 / 16	17 / 18	19 / 20	21 / 22	23 / 24	25 / 26	27 / 28	29 / 30	31 / ♑	1 / 2	3 / 4	5 / 6	7 / 8	9 / 10	11 / 12	13 / 14	31
IANVAR:	15 / 16	17 / 19	20 / 21	22 / 23	24 / 25	31 / ♒	1 / 2	3 / 4	5 / 6	7 / 8	9 / 10	11 / 12	13 / 14	15 / 16	17 / 18	19 / 20	31
FEBRVAR	24 / 25	26 / 27	28 / 29	30 / 31	♓ / 1	2 / 3	4 / 5	6 / 7	8 / 9	10 / 11	12 / 13	14 / 15	16 / 17	18 / 19			28
DIES.	1 / 2	3 / 4	5 / 6	7 / 8	9 / 10	11 / 12	13 / 14	15 / 16	17 / 18	19 / 20	21 / 22	23 / 24	25 / 26	27 / 28	29 / 30	31	

TABELLA SIGNVM GRADVMQVE SOLIS INDICANS.

32

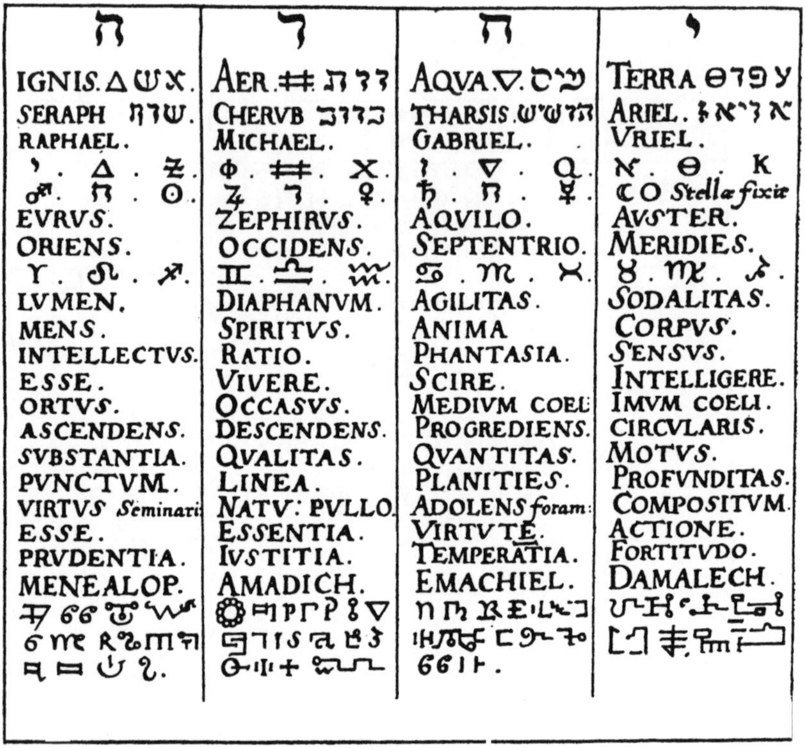

ה	ו	ה	י
IGNIS. △ אש.	AER. ⌗ רוח	AQVA. ▽. מים	TERRA 🜃 עפר
SERAPH שרף.	CHERVB כרוב	THARSIS. תרשיש	ARIEL. אריאל
RAPHAEL.	MICHAEL.	GABRIEL.	VRIEL.
י. △. ♃.	Φ. ⌗. X.	?. ▽. Q.	א. Θ. K
♂. ה. ☉.	♃. ו. ♀.	♄. ה. ☿.	☾ O Stellæ fixæ
EVRVS.	ZEPHIRVS.	AQVILO.	AVSTER.
ORIENS.	OCCIDENS.	SEPTENTRIO.	MERIDIES.
♈. ♌. ♐.	♊. ♎. ♒.	♋. ♏. ♓.	♉. ♍. ♑.
LVMEN.	DIAPHANVM.	AGILITAS.	SODALITAS.
MENS.	SPIRITVS.	ANIMA	CORPVS.
INTELLECTVS.	RATIO.	PHANTASIA.	SENSVS.
ESSE.	VIVERE.	SCIRE.	INTELLIGERE.
ORTVS.	OCCASVS.	MEDIVM COELI	IMVM COELI.
ASCENDENS.	DESCENDENS.	PROGREDIENS.	CIRCVLARIS.
SVBSTANTIA.	QVALITAS.	QVANTITAS.	MOTVS.
PVNCTVM.	LINEA.	PLANITIES.	PROFVNDITAS.
VIRTVS Seminari	NATV: PVLLO.	ADOLENS foram:	COMPOSITVM.
ESSE.	ESSENTIA.	VIRTVTE.	ACTIONE.
PRVDENTIA.	IVSTITIA.	TEMPERATIA.	FORTITVDO.
MENEALOP.	AMADICH.	EMACHIEL.	DAMALECH.
[illegible]	[illegible]	[illegible]	[illegible]

The Quaternary, the root and foundation of the numbers, the fount of Nature, containing the perfect number.

FOUR

The four lettered Name of God: Tetragrammaton

	ה	ו	ה	י
Four Elements[3]	Fire	Air	Water	Earth
Four Governors of the Elements	Seraph	Cherub	Tharsis	Ariel
Four Angels[4]	Raphael	Michael	Gabriel	Uriel
Hebrew and Greek Letters[5]	י △ Z ♂ ה ☉	ϕ #X ♃ ו ♀	ו ▽ Q ♄ ה ☿	א ⊖ K ☽ ○ fixed stars
Four Winds	Eurus	Zephirus	Aquilo	Auster
Four Points of the Compass	East	West	North	South
Four Zodiacal Triplicities	♈ ♌ ♐	♊ ♎ ♒	♋ ♏ ♓	♉ ♍ ♑
Four Elemental Qualities	Luminosity	Transparency	Mobility	Solidity [Soliditas]
Four Elements of Man	Mind	Spirit	Soul	Body
Four Powers of the Soul	Intellect	Reason	Imagination	Perception
Four Stages in the Ladder of Existence	to be	to live	to know	to understand
Four Points of Heaven	Rising point Ascendant	Setting point Descendant	Mid Heaven Zenith	Lowest point Nadir
Four Movements in Nature	Ascending	Descending	Proceeding	Revolving
Four Fundamentals of Nature	Substance	Quality	Quantity	Motion
Four Fundamentals of Mathematics	Point	Line	Plane	Volume
Four Fundamentals of the Physical	Life force of seed	Germination of Nature	Growth maturity	Completion and fruiting
Four Fundamentals of the Metaphysical	Being	Essence	Virtue	Action
Four Moral Virtues	Wisdom	Justice	Temperance	Courage
Four Spirits of Theophrastus (with Characters)	Menealop 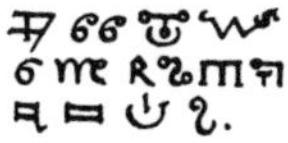	Amadich 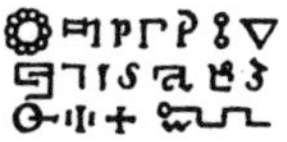	Emachiel 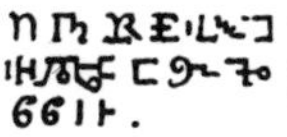	Damalech 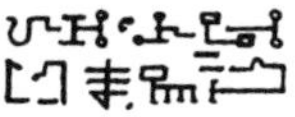

J	O	V ·	A
COLERA △	SANGVIS ⋕	PITVITA ▽	MELANCHO:
IMPETVS.	ALACRITAS.	INERTIA.	TARDITAS.
ÆSTAS.	VER.	HIEMS.	AVTVMNVS.
CASMARAN.	TALVI.	FARLAS.	ARDARAEL.
GARGATEL.	CARACASA.	AMABAEL.	TARQVAM.
TARIEL.	AMATIEL.	CTARARI.	GVALBAREL
TVBIEL. 2	COMISOROS.		
GAVIEL. 1	SPVGLIGVEL.	ALTARIB.	TORQVARET.
FESTATVI.	AMADAI.	GERENIA.	RABIANIRA.
MARCVS.	IOANNES.	MATTHÆVS.	LVCAS.
LEO.	AQVILA.	HOMO.	VITVLVS.
ANIMALIA.	PLANTÆ.	METALLA.	LAPIDES.
PROGRESSIVA.	VOLATILIA.	NATANTIA.	REPTILIA.
SEMINA.	FLORES.	FOLIA.	RADICES.
CALIDVM.	HVMIDVM.	FRIGIDVM.	SICCVM.
☉ ♂	♀ ♃	☿	♄ ☽
AVRVM ♂	CVPRVMSTAN.	ARGENT: VIVV:	PLVMB: ARGEN:
LVCENTES.	LEVES Transparent.	CLAR: CONG:	GRAVES Opaci.
THAAR. ♈	CONFOR. ♊	BASAN. ♋	PANTHEON. ♉
CORONA ♌	ERROR. ♎	ZARNECH ♏	ERIM. ♍
HERMON ♐	SAFFOR. ♒	ELISAN ♓	NAIM. ♑
BAEL.	MOYMON.	POYMON.	EGIN.
SILPPHANI.	AEREI.	NIMPHÆ.	PIGMEI.

	J	O	V	A
Four Humors[5]	Choleric △ Yellow Bile	Sanguine # Blood	Phlegmatic ▽ Phlegm	Melancholy ⊖ Black Bile
Four Habits	Passionate	Lively	Inactive	Dull
Four Seasons	Summer	Spring	Winter	Autumn
Names of the Four Seasons[6]	Casmaran	Talvi	Farlas	Ardarael
Angels of the Four Seasons[6]	Gargatel Tariel Gaviel	Caracasa Amatiel Comisoros	Amabael Ctarari	Tarquam Gualbarel
Rulers of the Signs of the Four Seasons[6]	Tubiel	Spugliguel	Altarib	Torquaret
Four Names of the Earth[6]	Festatui	Amadai	Gerenia	Rabianira
Four Evangelists	Mark	John	Matthew	Luke
Four Sacred Animals	Lion	Eagle	Man	Bull
Four Species	Animals	Plants	Metals	Stones
Four Kinds of Animal	Crawling	Winged	Swimming	Creeping
Four Elementary Correspondences in Plants	Seeds	Flowers	Leaves	Roots
Four Qualities	Hot	Wet	Cold	Dry
Four Elementary Correspondences in Metals	☉ Gold ♂ Iron	♀ Copper ♃ Tin	☿ Quicksilver	♄ Lead ☽ Silver
Four Elementary Correspondences in Stones	Shining Glittering	Polished Transparent	Clear Hard	Heavy Opaque
Four Sublime Celestial Signs	Thaar ♈ Corona ♌ Hermon ♐	Confor ♊ Error ♎ Saffor ♒	Basan ♋ Zarnech ♏ Elisan ♓	Pantheon ♉ Erim ♍ Naim ♑
Principal Spirits in the Four Parts of the World[7, 31]	Bael	Moymon	Poymon	Egin
Spirits of the Four Elements[8]	Sylphs	Aerei	Nymphs	Pigmies

ה	ו	ש	ה	י
VULNERA.	IHESV.	CHRISTI	SALVATORIS	NOSTRI.
AQVA.	AER.	IGNIS	TERRA.	MIXTVM.
VEGETATIVA.	SENSITIVA.	CONCVPISCIBILIS.	IRASCIBILIS.	RATIONALIS.
VISVS.	AVDITVS.	OLFACTVS.	GVSTVS.	TACTVS.
SATVRNVS.	IVPITER.	MARS.	VENVS.	MERCVRIVS.
LAPIDES.	METALLA.	PLANTÆ.	ZOOPHYTA.	ANIMALIA.
HOMINES.	QVATRVPEDIA.	REPTILIA.	NATANTIA.	VOLATILIA.

FIVE

Five lettered Name of God: Ihesuh

	ה	ו	ש	ה	י
Five	wounds	of Jesus	Christ	the Savior	of us
Five Corrupt Species	Water	Air	Fire	Earth	Mixed
Five Vain Powers	Vigor	Sensation	Coveting	Anger	Calculating
Five Senses	Sight	Hearing	Smell	Taste	Touch
Five Wandering Stars	Saturn	Jupiter	Mars	Venus	Mercury
Five Mixed Species	Stones	Metals	Plants	Zoophytes	Animals
Five Animal Species	Man	Quadrupeds	Reptiles	Sea creatures	Winged creatures

The Quinary, the half of the Denary, consisting of even and odd like male and female, sacred to Mercury.

The Chiromancy of the Left Hand

The Right Hand Containing the Twelve Signs

The Human Figure Containing the Planets

The Image of Man Comprising the Twelve Signs

ו	ו	ב
SERAPHIM.	CHERVBIN.	THRONI.
SATVRNVS.	IVPITER.	MARS.
ARCTICVS.	ANTARCTICVS.	TROPICVS.
MAGNITVDO.	COLOR.	FIGVRA.
QVIES.	RARITAS.	ACVITAS.
INTELLECTVS.	MEMORIA.	SENSVS.
LVNÆ.	MARTIS.	MERCVRII.
ANTE.	RETRO.	SVRSVM.
SEXTO	DIE	CHRISTVS.
SEXTO	DIE	HOMO.

SENARIVS PERFECTIONIS, REDEMPTIONIS ET

The six lettered Name of God: El Gibor

	ר	ו	ב
Six Orders of Angels	Seraphim	Cherubim	Thrones
Six Planets	Saturn	Jupiter	Mars
Six Circles on the Globe	Arctic	Antarctic	Tropic
Six Characteristics of a Lump of Matter	Size	Color	Shape
Six Qualities of Substance	Rest	Thinness	Sharpness
Six Grades in Man	Intellect	Memory	Perception
Six Wandering Planets	Moon	Mars	Mercury
Six Different Positions	Before	Behind	Above
	On the sixth	Day	Christ . . .
	On the sixth	Day	Man . . .

The Senary is called the number of perfection, of the redemption, and of Man.

ג	ב	א
DOMINATIONES.	POTESTATES.	VIRTVTES.
VENVS.	MERCVRIVS.	LVNA.
TROPICVS.	ÆQVINOCTIALIS.	ECLYPTVS.
INTERVALLVM	STATVS.	MOTVS.
OBTVSITAS.	DENSITAS.	MOTVS.
MOTVS.	VITA.	ESSENTIA.
IOVIS.	VENERIS.	SATVRNI.
DEO[s]RVM.	DEXTRORSVM	SINISTRORVM.
PRO REDEM[p]TIONE	HVMANA.	PASSVS EST.
A DEO.	CREATVS.	EST.

HOMINIS NVMERVS APPELLATVR.

SIX

	ג	ל	א
Six Orders of Angels	Dominions	Powers	Virtues
Six Planets	Venus	Mercury	Moon
Six Circles on the Globe	Tropic	Equator	Ecliptic
Six Character-istics of a Lump of Matter	Distance	Position	Motion
Six Qualities of Substance	Bluntness	Density	Motion
Six Grades in Man	Will	Life	Essence
Six Wandering Planets	Jupiter	Venus	Saturn
Six Different Positions	Below	Right	Left
	. . . suffered	for the redemption of humanity	
	. . . was created	by God	

No:	Vr	IANVAR		FEBRVAR		MARTIVS		APRILIS		MAIVS		IVNIVS.	
		Ortus	Occas	Ortus	Occas	Ortus	Occasus	Ortus	Occasus	Ortus	Occasus	Ortus	Occasus
1	22	752	448	75	453	618	543	521	639	431	729	359	81
2	23	751	409	76	454	616	544	518	641	430	730	359	81
3	24	750	410	74	456	615	545	517	643	429	731	359	81
4	25	749	411	72	458	614	547	515	645	427	733	358	82
5	26	748	412	71	459	611	549	514	646	426	734	358	82
6	27	747	413	659	51	69	551	512	648	424	736	358	82
7	28	746	414	657	53	67	553	510	650	423	737	358	82
8	29	745	415	655	55	66	554	59	652	422	739	358	82
9	30	744	416	653	57	64	557	58	654	420	740	358	82
10	31	742	418	652	58	62	558	55	655	419	741	357	83
11	1	741	419	650	510	60	60	53	657	418	742	357	83
12	2	740	420	648	512	558	62	52	659	417	743	357	83
13	3	738	422	646	514	556	64	51	71	416	744	357	83
14	4	737	423	644	516	554	66	459	73	415	745	358	82
15	5	735	425	643	517	552	68	457	75	414	746	358	82
16	6	732	426	641	519	551	69	455	76	413	747	358	82
17	7	731	428	640	521	549	611	454	78	412	748	358	82
18	8	730	429	637	523	547	613	452	79	411	749	358	82
19	9	728	430	635	525	545	615	451	711	410	750	358	82
20	10	727	432	633	527	544	616	449	713	49	751	359	81
21	11	725	433	632	528	542	618	447	715	48	752	359	80
22	12	724	435	630	530	540	620	444	716	47	753	359	80
23	13	722	436	628	532	538	622	442	718	46	754	359	759
24	14	721	438	626	533	536	624	440	720	45	755	40	758
25	15	719	439	628	534	534	626	439	723	44	756	340	759
26	16	718	441	624	536	532	628	436	723	43	75	41	759
27	17	710	442	622	538	530	630	437	724	43	75	42	758
28	18	714	444	620	540	528	632	434	650	42	758	43	757
29	19	713	446			526	634	433	726	41	759	44	757
30	20	711	447			525	635	432	727	40	70	44	756
31	21	712	449			523	637			40	70		

Ivllius		Avgvst,		Septem:		Octobe.		Novembr.		Decemb:	
Ortg.	Occasg	Ortg.	Occasg	Ortg.	Occasg	Ortg.	Occasg	Ortg.	Occasg	Ortg:	Occasg
45	755	444	716	538	622	632	528	725	435	80	40
46	754	445	715	540	620	633	527	727	433	81	40
47	753	447	713	542	618	635	525	728	432	81	359
48	752	449	711	544	616	637	523	730	430	82	359
49	751	451	79	545	615	638	520	731	429	82	358
410	750	452	78	547	613	641	519	732	428	82	358
411	749	454	76	547	611	643	517	734	426	82	358
412	748	455	75	551	69	644	516	735	425	82	358
413	747	457	73	552	68	646	514	737	423	83	358
414	746	459	71	554	66	648	512	738	422	83	358
415	745	51	659	556	64	650	510	740	420	83	357
416	744	53	657	558	62	652	58	741	419	83	357
417	743	55	655	60	60	653	57	742	418	83	357
418	742	56	654	62	558	655	55	744	416	82	357
419	741	57	653	63	557	656	52	745	415	82	357
420	740	58	651	64	556	659	51	746	414	82	358
421	739	510	650	66	554	72	459	747	413	82	358
423	737	512	648	67	553	72	458	748	412	83	358
424	736	514	646	69	551	74	456	749	411	81	358
426	734	515	645	611	549	76	454	750	410	81	358
427	733	517	643	613	547	77	453	751	49	80	359
429	731	519	641	615	545	79	451	752	48	80	359
430	730	521	639	616	544	711	449	754	46	80	40
431	729	523	637	618	542	713	447	755	45	759	40
433	727	525	635	620	540	714	446	756	44	758	42
434	726	526	634	622	538	716	444	756	44	757	43
436	724	528	632	624	536	718	442	757	43	756	44
437	723	530	630	626	534	719	441	758	42	756	44
439	721	532	628	628	532	721	439	759	41	755	46
440	720	534	626	629	530	722	438	759	41	754	46
442	710	536	624			724	436			753	47

This is one of the three purely astronomical tables found in the Magical Calendar. *It is an ephemeris of the rising and setting times of the Sun throughout the year. The days of the months are given on the right hand side, in both the new and the old calendar system, which were eleven days apart. During the late sixteenth century the calendrical system was revised. The Julian system which had been used since Roman times and had been cumulatively getting out of step with the cycle of the seasons, was replaced by a new Gregorian system, necessitating the loss of eleven days. This Gregorian Calendar was introduced in 1582 by Pope Gregory XIII, and was almost immediately accepted in Catholic countries, though it was more slowly adopted in Protestant countries, and in some areas survived into the eighteenth century. Indeed, even today we find in some eastern European countries that Church festivals are still fixed by the old calendar.*

SPIRITVS SAPIENTIÆ.
ZAPHKIEL.
ARATRON.
SATVRNVS.
CASSIEL.
SATVRNI domus est noctis diei
Huic dolor est Gloria Seni.
imago.
ALBVMASARIS.
SANITAS
CONTRIS
DOLOR
VITA

The seven lettered Name of God: Ararita

א

Seven Gifts of the Holy Spirit[9]	Spirit of Wisdom
Seven Angels Standing Near God	Zaphkiel צפקיאל
Seven Spirits of the Planets[10]	Aratron 
Seven Planets	Saturn ♄ ♑ ♒
Seven Angels of the Planets[11]	Cassiel 
Houses of Exaltation and Decline of the Seven Planets	Saturn's House is: of night ♑, of day ♒ In ♈ there is trouble, in ♎ glory.
Sigils of the Seven Planets[12]	
Characters of the Seven Planets[13]	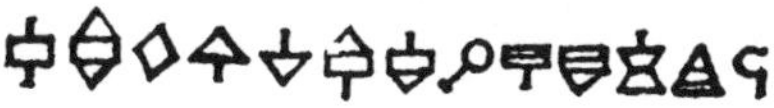
Divine Letters of the Seven Planets	
Seven Onomantic Tables[14]	Albumasar

The Septenary, the vehicle of human life, the most complete number full of every power, sacred to the Holy Spirit.

SPIRITVS INTELLIGENTIÆ.
ZADKIEL.
BETOR.
IVPITER.
SACHIEL.
IVPITER arcitenēs tenet cum
Cui in sors, mala iniquo
EM.
PYTHAGORÆ.
MEDIVM
VITA
SPES
MORS
ÆGRITV
PERICVL
Ætatem

SEVEN

ח

Seven Gifts of the Holy Spirit[9]	Spirit of Intelligence
Seven Angels Standing Near God	Zadkiel צדקיאל
Seven Spirits of the Planets[10]	Betor 
Seven Planets	Jupiter ♃ ♐ ♓
Seven Angels of the Planets[11]	Sachiel 
Houses of Exaltation and Decline of the Seven Planets	Jupiter holds the archer, ♐, with ♓ when in ♋, fortune, ill luck in ♉
Sigils of the Seven Planets[12]	
Characters of the Seven Planets[13]	
Divine Letters of the Seven Planets	
Seven Onomantic Tables[14]	Pythagoras

ר
SPIRITVS CONSILII.
CAMAEL. כמאל
PHALEC.
MARS.
SAMAEL.
Sed MARTIS domus est ♈ & ♏ pugnax
Huncque ♄ tollit ♋ ad ima premit.
PTOLOMEI.
MEDIVM
FORTVN
MEDIVM
MORS.
INFORTV
VITA.

ז

Seven Gifts of the Holy Spirit[9]	Spirit of Judgment
Seven Angels Standing Near God	Camael כמאל
Seven Spirits of the Planets[10]	Phalec 
Seven Planets	Mars ♂ ♈ ♏
Seven Angels of the Planets[11]	Samael 
Houses of Exaltation and Decline of the Seven Planets	The house of Mars is ♈ and aggressive ♏ This is removed in ♑, and pressed lowest in ♋
Sigils of the Seven Planets[12]	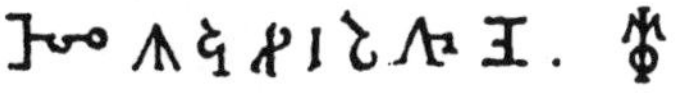
Characters of the Seven Planets[13]	
Divine Letters of the Seven Planets	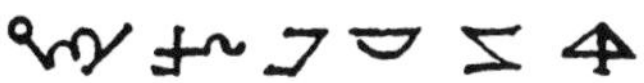
Seven Onomantic Tables[14]	Ptolemy

ר
SPIRITVS FORTITVDINIS.
RAPHAEL רפאל
OCH.
SOL.
ANAEL.
SOL tene hospiciū sibi Sol in æde
Atq illi est gloria dolor.
ANTHIDONIS.
Ætatem
MEDIVM
DVBIVM
MORS
MEDIVM
INFORTV
VITA

ר

Seven Gifts of the Holy Spirit[9]	Spirit of Courage
Seven Angels Standing Near God	Raphael רפאל
Seven Spirits of the Planets[10]	Och 
Seven Planets	Sun ☉ ♌
Seven Angels of the Planets[11]	Anael 
Houses of Exaltation and Decline of the Seven Planets	The Sun is at home only in the house of ♌ And in ♈ there is glory, in ♎ sorrow.
Sigils of the Seven Planets[12]	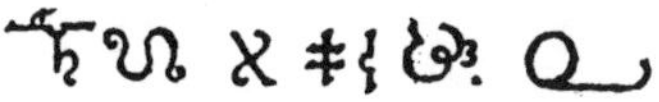
Characters of the Seven Planets[13]	
Divine Letters of the Seven Planets	
Seven Onomantic Tables[14]	Anthidonus

א
SPIRITVS SCIENTIÆ.
HANIEL. האניאל
HAGIT
VENVS.
RAPHAEL.
AtVEN, in per atria versat.
exultat pressa iacet.
PLATONIS.
MEDIVM
FORTVM
MEDIV
MORS.
INFORTV
VITA

א

Seven Gifts of the Holy Spirit[9]	Spirit of Science
Seven Angels Standing Near God	Hanael האניאל
Seven Spirits of the Planets[10]	Hagit 
Seven Planets	Venus ♀ ♉ ♎
Seven Angels of the Planets[11]	Raphael 
Houses of Exaltation and Decline of the Seven Planets	Venus dwells in the houses of ♉ and ♎ In ♓ it is exalted in ♍ it lies subdued
Sigils of the Seven Planets[12]	
Characters of the Seven Planets[13]	
Divine Letters of the Seven Planets	
Seven Onomantic Tables[14]	Plato

Spiritus Pietatis.
Michael.
Ophiel
Mercurius.
Michael.
Aristotelis.
VITA
FOR TVN
SANITAS
MORS
MOR BOS
ADVERS

ז

Seven Gifts of the Holy Spirit[9]	Spirit of Affection
Seven Angels Standing Near God	Michael מיכאל
Seven Spirits of the Planets[10]	Ophiel 
Seven Planets	Mercury ☿ ♊ ♍
Seven Angels of the Planets[11]	Michael 
Houses of Exaltation and Decline of the Seven Planets	Mercury dwelling in ♊ triumphs on his throne. It is afflicted in ♍ and comes to its head in ♓
Sigils of the Seven Planets[12]	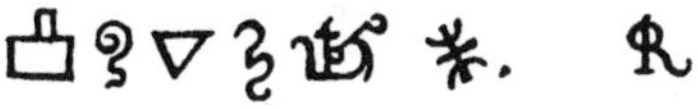
Characters of the Seven Planets[13]	
Divine Letters of the Seven Planets	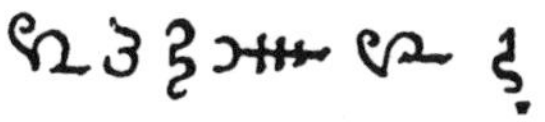
Seven Onomantic Tables[14]	Aristotle

א

SPIRITVS TIMORIS.

GABRIEL. גבריאל

PHVL.

LVNA. ♋

GABRIEL.

LVNA domum ♋ tenet illam ♉ honorat Et super hanc versans ♏ sorte premit.

HALI.

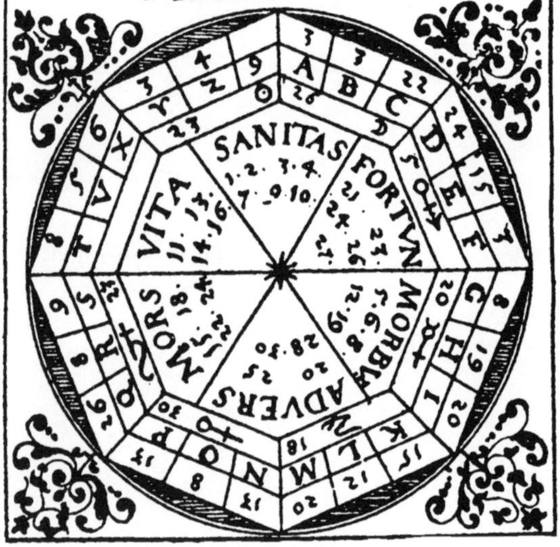

SEVEN

א

Seven Gifts of the Holy Spirit[9]	Spirit of Fear
Seven Angels Standing Near God	Gabriel גבריאל
Seven Spirits of the Planets[10]	Phul 
Seven Planets	Moon ☽ ♋
Seven Angels of the Planets[11]	Gabriel 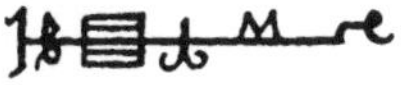
Houses of Exaltation and Decline of the Seven Planets	The Moon possesses ♋ It honors ♉, and moreover its fortune is subdued in ♏
Sigils of the Seven Planets[12]	
Characters of the Seven Planets[13]	
Divine Letters of the Seven Planets	
Seven Onomantic Tables[14]	Hales

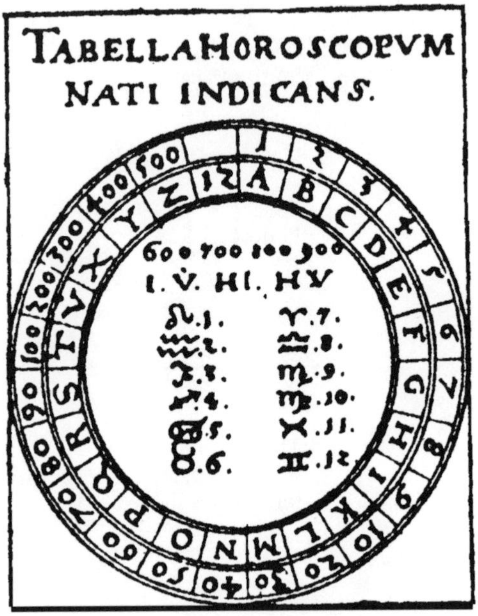

Table Indicating the Horoscope of Birth[19]

SEVEN

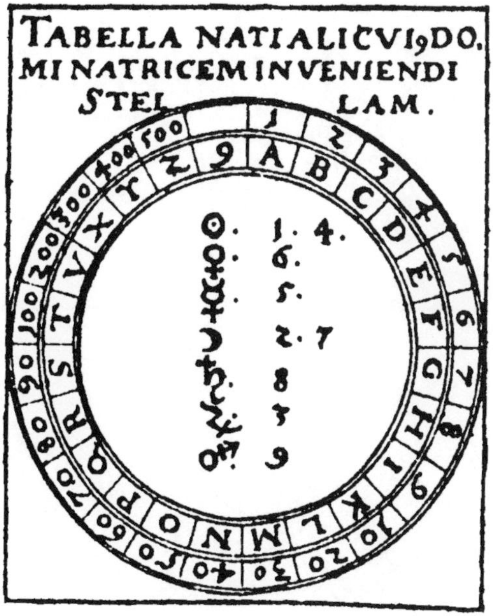

Table for Finding Out from One's Birthday the Ruling Stars of the House[19]

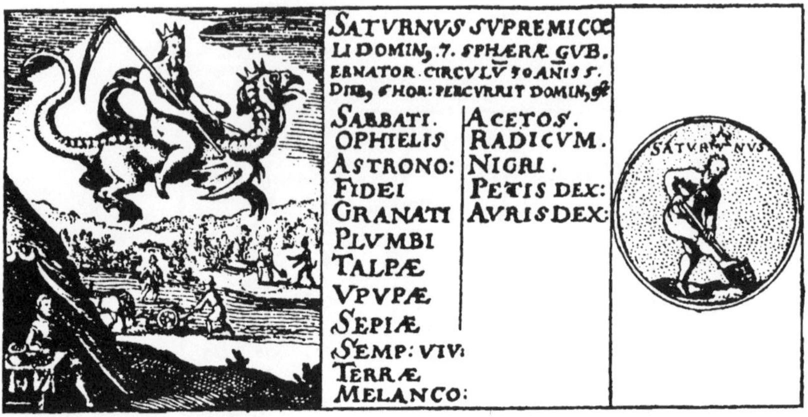
SATVRNVS SVPREMI CŒ
LI DOMIN, 7. SPHÆRÆ GVB.
ERNATOR. CIRCVLV̄ 30 ANIS 5.
DIEB, 6 HOR: PERCVRRIT DOMIN,
SABBATI.
OPHIELIS
ASTRONO:
FIDEI
GRANATI
PLVMBI
TALPÆ
VPVPÆ
SEPIÆ
SEMP: VIV:
TERRÆ
MELANCO:
ACETOS.
RADICVM.
NIGRI.
PETIS DEX:
AVRIS DEX:
SATVRNVS

15

16

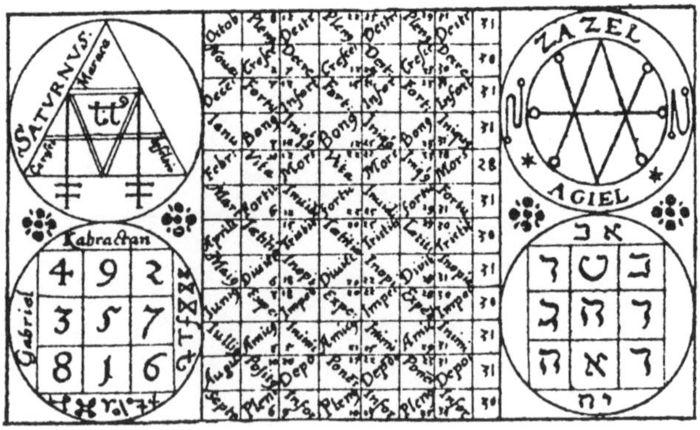
SATVRNVS
Kabractan
4 9 2
3 5 7
8 1 6
Gabriel
ZAZEL
AGIEL

17, 18

SEVEN

Saturn, the master of the highest heaven, the governor of the seventh sphere, travels through his circuit in 30 years, 5 days, 6 hours.

He is master of:

Saturday	Acid
Ophiel	Roots
Astronomy	Black
Faith	Right Foot
Granite	Right Ear
Lead	
Moles	
Lapwing	
Cuttlefish	
Sempervivum	
Earth	
Black Bile	

Saturn, crowned and complete with sickle, rides a fearsome crowned winged dragon. Below a landowner sits in a tent, while his workers plough and sow the land. In the background a figure standing within a circle seems to be menaced by a demonic being.

Table of fortunate and unfortunate days for Saturn

Plenus	-	full, complete	Laetitia	-	joy, exuberance
Destr	-	destruction	Tristit	-	sorrow
Cresce	-	growing	Diviti	-	wealth
Decre	-	diminishing	Inopia	-	poverty
Bonus	-	good	Exped	-	expedient
Iniquo	-	unfavourable	Imped	-	impediment, hindrance
Vita	-	life	Amicus	-	friendship
Mors	-	death	Inimi	-	enmity
Fortu	-	fortunate	Positus	-	establish
Infort	-	unfortunate	Pones	-	set up
Invidi	-	hostility, envy	Depones	-	give up

IVPI TER
IVPITER IN COELO Z RE
GNANS SPHÆRAM 6 IN
HABITAT ILLAM XI. ANNIS
PERCVRRIT AMAT.
IOVIS DIEM DVLCES
ZACHANI: FRVCTVS
RHETORICA: CÆRVLE.
SPEM. CAPVT.
TOPASIVM: AVREM SIN:
STAGNVM.
CERVVM.
AQVILAM.
DELPHIN:
BARB:IOV:
ÆRA
SANGVIN:

15

16

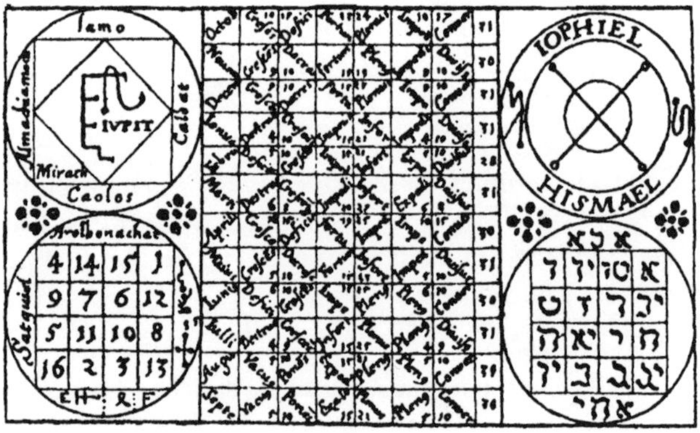
Iamo
IVPIT
Mirach
Caolos
4 14 15 1
9 7 6 12
5 11 10 8
16 2 3 13
IOPHIEL
HISMAEL

17, 18

SEVEN

Jupiter, reigning in the second heaven, inhabits the sixth sphere, which he travels through in 12 years.

He loves:

Thursday	Sweet
Zachani	Fruits
Rhetoric	Blue
Hope	Head
Topaz	Left Ear
Tin	
Deer	
Eagle	
Dolphin	
Jove's Beard (Silver-leaved Woodblade plant)	
Air	
Blood	

Jupiter, crowned and brandishing his bundle of thunderbolts, flies above on a magnificent winged stag. Below in the forest around an impressive town, a hunt is taking place.

Table of fortunate and unfortunate days for Jupiter

Cresce	growth	Decres	diminishing
Defici	decline	Destruo	destruction
Fortum	fortunate	Infor	unfortunate
Plenus	full, complete	Expedi	expedient
Impedi	hindrance	Vacuo	empty
Conver	reverse	Pones	establish
Divisus	separated, divided	Exalto	raised

MARS RECTOR CŒLI
♂. IN SPHÆRA ♂ CVRSVM
SVVM 2 ANNIS ABSOLVIT
ET REGIT.
DIE: MART:
SAMAELEM
GEOMETRI:
FORTITVD:
RVBINVM.
FERRVM.
LVPVM.
VULTVREM.
LVCIVM.
NAPELLVM.
CHOLERAM.
IGNEM.
AMAROS:
LIGN: SAND.
RVBEOS.
MAN: DEX:
NAR: DEX:
MARS

15

16

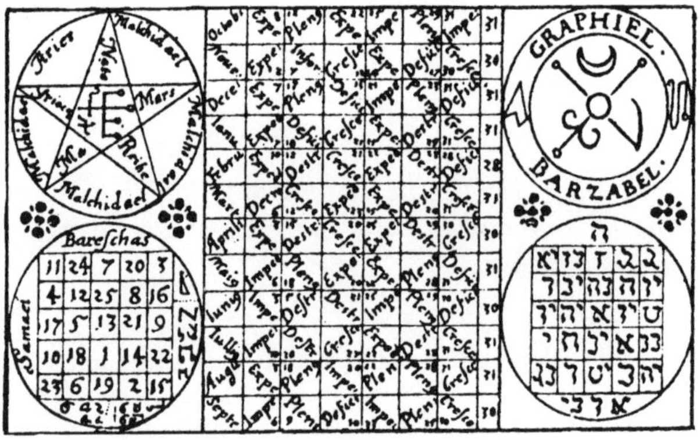
GRAPHIEL
BARZABEL
Bareschas
Malchidael
Aries
Mars

17, 18

SEVEN

Mars, ruler of the third heaven, completes his course through the fifth sphere in 2 years.

He rules:

Tuesday	Bitter
Samael	Sandalwood
Geometry	Red
Strength	Right hand
Ruby	Right nostril
Iron	
Wolf	
Vulture	
Pike	
Monkshood	
Choler, Yellow Bile	
Fire	

Mars, brandishing sword and shield, stands beside a fierce lion rampant. In the background a battle is taking place with soldiers lined up and laying siege to a castle which is in flames.

Table of fortunate and unfortunate days for Mars

Plenus	-	full, complete	Cresce	-	growing
Impe	-	hindrance	Defici	-	decline
Exped	-	expedient	Destr	-	destruction
Infor	-	unfortunate	Decre	-	diminishing

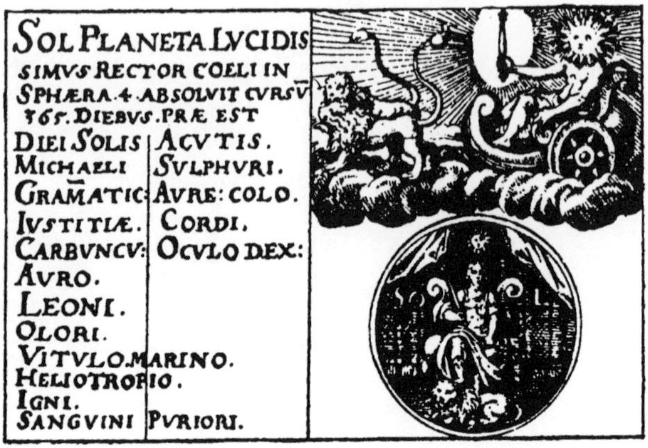
SOL PLANETA LVCIDIS
SIMVS RECTOR COELI IN
SPHÆRA. 4. ABSOLVIT CVRSV
365. DIEBVS. PRÆ EST
DIEI SOLIS ACVTIS.
MICHAELI SVLPHVRI.
GRAMATIC: AVRE: COLO.
IVSTITIÆ. CORDI.
CARBVNCV: OCVLO DEX:
AVRO.
LEONI.
OLORI.
VITVLO.MARINO.
HELIOTROPIO.
IGNI.
SANGVINI PVRIORI.

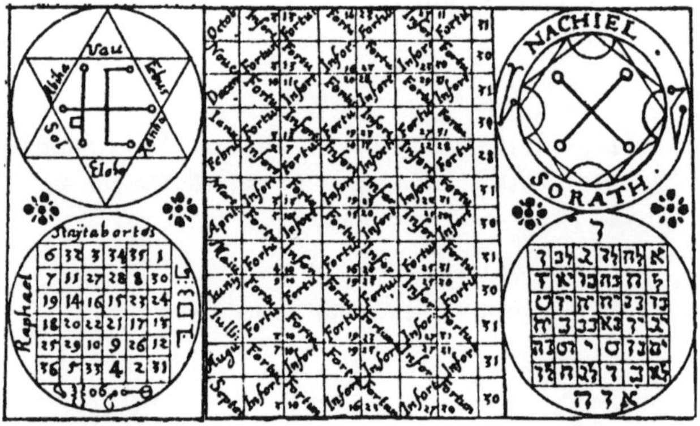
NACHIEL.
SORATH.

15 17, 18

16

SEVEN

The Sun, the brightest planet, rules the fourth heaven. He completes his course in the fourth sphere in 365 days.

He commands:

Sunday	Sharp
Michael	Sulphur
Grammar	Golden color
Justice	Heart
Carbuncle	Right eye
Gold	
Lion	
Swan	
The sea cow	
Heliotrope	
Fire	
Pure blood	

Sol, holding in his right hand a sceptre of power, is drawn in his chariot by two lions.

Table of fortunate and unfortunate days for the Sun

Fortu - Fortunate Infortu - unfortunate

VE NVS
VENVS REGNAT IN COE
LO 5. SPHERA 3 ABSOLVENS
CVRSVM SVVM 350 DIEBVS
SVBEST DIES.
VENERIS.
ANAEL.
MVSICA.
CHARITAS
SMARACTVS
CVPRVM.
HIRCVS.
COLVMBA.
THIMALLVS.
CAPILLVM VENERIS.
AER
PITVITA CVM SANGVI:
DVLCIS.
FLOS.
VIRIDIS.
PVDENT?
NARIS SINI

15

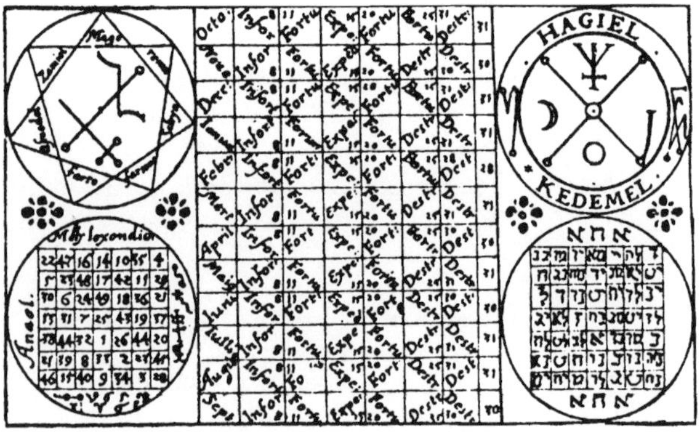
HAGIEL
KEDEMEL
Anael

17, 18

16

SEVEN

Venus rules in the fifth heaven, completing her course through the third sphere in 350 days.

Beneath her is the day:

Friday	Sweet
Anael	Flowers
Music	Green
Love	Sex organs
Emerald	Left nostril
Copper	
Billy goat	
Dove	
Thimallus	
Maidenhair	
Air	
Phlegm with blood	

Venus is shown here together with a winged cherub or Eros holding a bow. She holds a flaming heart in her left hand. Above a group of birds are flying.

Table of fortunate and unfortunate days for Venus

Fortu	-	fortunate	Exped	-	expedient
Infor	-	unfortunate	Destr	-	destruction

MERCVRIVS COELVM .6.
SPHERAM 2 COLIT CVRSV
358 DIEBVS PERAGENS. SVNT
MERCVRIALIA:
DIES MERCURII
RAPHAEL.
ARITMETICA.
TEMPERANT.
CRISTALLVM.
MERCVR. VIV.
SIMIA
CICONIA
TROCHVS.
HERB: MERC:
AQVA.
SPIRIT. AIA.
VARIVS PERM.
CORTEX.
OMN: COLOR
MAN, SIN
OS.

15

16

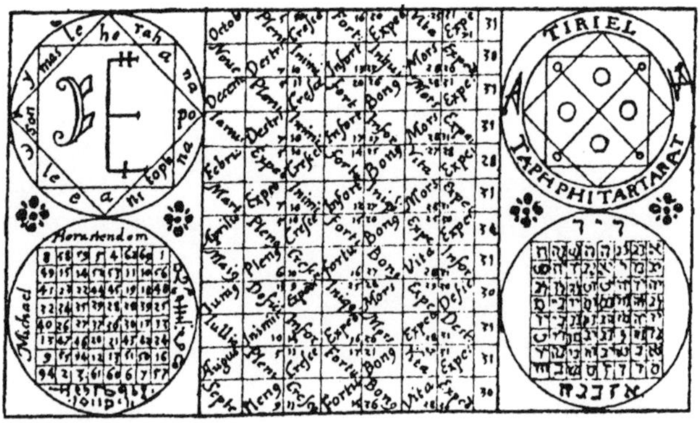
TIRIEL
TAPHPHITARTARAT
Michael

17, 18

SEVEN

Mercury inhabits the sixth heaven, passing through his course in the second sphere in 358 days.

The Mercurial things are:

Wednesday	Various mixtures
Raphael	Bark
Arithmetic	All colors
Temperance	Left hand
Crystal	Mouth
Quicksilver	
Apes	
Stork	
Trout	
Herbs of Mercury	
Water	
Spirit, Soul	

Mercury in his winged sandals and helmet, holding the caduceus and an open book, flies above the figure of a man taking measurements of the angle to the top of a church spire. Nearby this figure are the tools of various crafts—saws, shovels, an alchemical still and crucibles, a palette and artist's brushes. In the background two men are leading a giraffe-like creature.

Table of fortunate and unfortunate days for Mercury

Plenus	-	full, complete	Infort	-	unfortunate
Cresce	-	growing, increasing	Iniqui	-	unfavourable
Fortu	-	fortunate	Mors	-	death
Exped	-	expedient	Bonus	-	good
Vita	-	life	Defici	-	failure, lack
Destr	-	destruction	Inimi	-	hostility

LVNA
LVNA REGINA COELI 7.
SPHÆRAM I. 27. DIEBVS. 7
HORIS 23 MINVT ABSOLV
IT ET SVNT LVNARIA.
LVNÆ DIES
GABRIEL.
DIALECTICA
PRVDENTIA
SAPHIRVS.
ARGENTVM
FELIS
NOCTVA.
ÆLVRVS.
SELENOTROPIA.
TERRA ET AQVA.
PITVITA.
SALSI.
VEGETATIV.
ALBVS.
PES SINIST.
OCVLVS SIN.

15

16

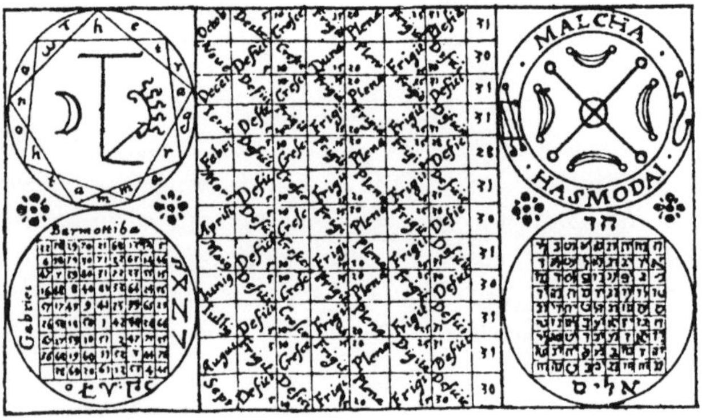
MALCHA
HASMODAI

17, 18

SEVEN

The Moon reigns in the seventh heaven, and completes her cycle of the first sphere in 27 days, 7 hours and 23 minutes.

These are of the Moon:

Monday	Salt
Gabriel	Leaves
Dialectic	White
Prudence	Left foot
Sapphire	Left eye
Silver	
Cat	
Owl	
Seal	
Selenotrope	
Earth and Water	
Phlegm	

The figure shows Luna as a goddess holding a torch and sitting upon a bull, prancing through the waves. Various sea creatures surround the figures and ships are seen in the background, where also a volcano erupts and a shooting star streaks earthwards past the Moon.

Table of fortunate and unfortunate days for the Moon

Destr	-	destruction	Plena	-	full, complete
Cresce	-	growing, increasing	Defici	-	failure, lack
Frigit	-	cold, chilling			

ח	ע	ז	ז
HÆREDITAS.	INCORRVPTIO.	POTESTAS.	VICTORIA.
PACIFICI.	ESVRIENTES.	MITES.	PERSECVTI.
COELVM STELLA:	SATVRNI.	IOVIS.	MERCVRII.
FOEMORALIA.	TVNICA.	CINGVLVS.	TYARA.
SICCITAS TERRÆ:	FRIGIDITAS AQV.	HVMIDI: AERIS.	CALIDIT: IGNIS.
ADÆ.	MOYSIS.	HELIÆ.	IOSVÆ.

EIGHT

The eight lettered Name of God: Tetragrammaton Vedaath

	ת	ע	ד	ו
Eight Gifts of the Beatitudes[20]	Inheritance	Wholeness	Power	Victory
Eight Types of the Beatitudes[20]	Peacemakers	Hungry	Meek	Persecuted
Eight Visible Heavens	Fixed Stars	Saturn	Jupiter	Mercury
Eight Ornaments of the Priests[33]	Foemoralia	Tunic	Girdle	Crown
Eight Divisions of the Qualities	Dryness of Earth	Coldness of Water	Wetness of Air	Warmth of Fire
Eight Most Sacred Tablets of the Fathers	Adam	Moses	Elias	Joshua

The Octonary denotes the number of Eternity, of the preservation of health.

ה	ד	ח	י
VISIODEI	GRATIA.	REGNVM.	GAVDIVM.
MVNDI CORDe	MISERICORDES	PAVPERES SPIRI:	LVGENTES.
SOLIS.	VENERIS.	MARTIS.	LVNÆ.
STOLATALAR.	SVPERHVMER.	RATIONALE.	LAMINA AVR:
CALIDIT: AERIS.	HVMIDIT AQVÆ	SICCITAS IGNIS	FRIGIDIT TERR:
EZECHIELIS.	DANIELIS.	SALOMON.	IEREMIÆ.

EIGHT

	ה	ו	ה	י
Eight Gifts of the Beatitudes[20]	Vision of God	Grace	Kingdom	Joy
Eight Types of the Beatitudes[20]	Pure in heart	Merciful	Poor in spirit	Mourners
Eight Visible Heavens	Sun	Venus	Mars	Moon
Eight Ornaments of the Priests[33]	Robe	Ephod	Rationale	Gold plate
Eight Divisions of the Qualities	Warmth of Air	Wetness of Water	Dryness of Fire	Coldness of Earth
Eight Most Sacred Tablets of the Fathers	Ezechiel	Daniel	Solomon	Jeremiah

Adam

Moses

Elias

Joshua

The Most Sacred Tablets of the Fathers[21]

EIGHT

Ezekiel

Daniel

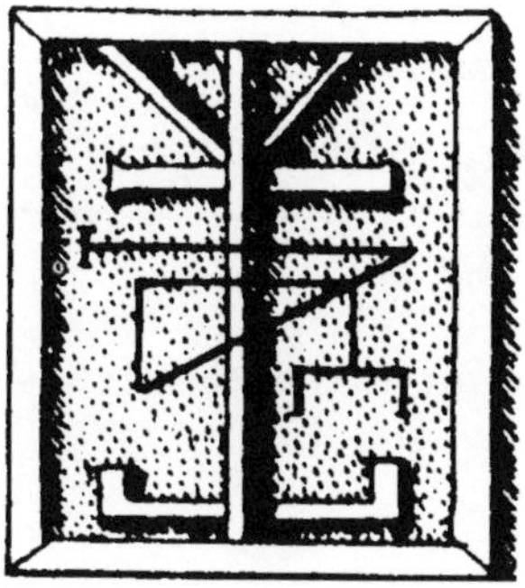

Solomon

Jeremiah

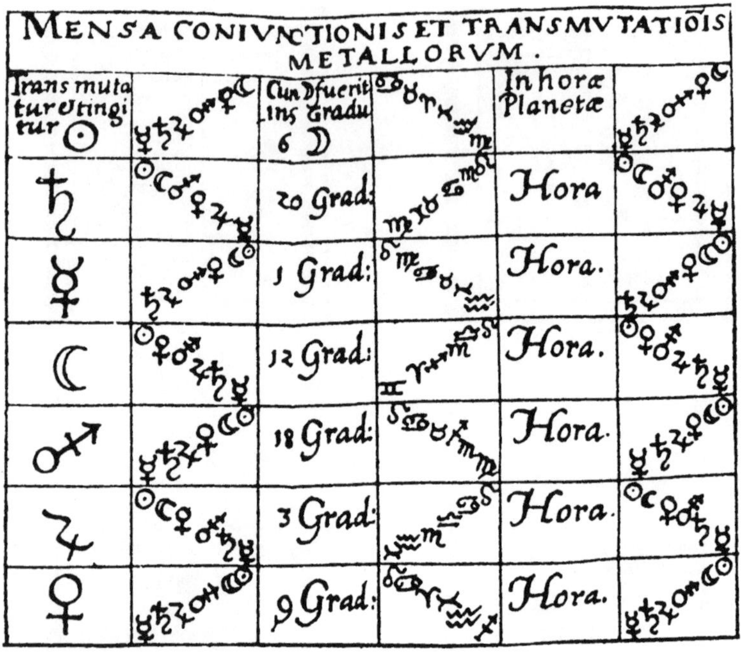

MENSA CONIVNCTIONIS ET TRANSMVTATIOĪS METALLORVM.					
Transmutatur & tingitur ☉	☿♄♃♂♀☾	Cum ☽ fuerit in ♋ Gradu 6 ☽	♋♉♈♐♒♍	In horæ Planetæ	☿♄♃♂♀☾
♄	☉☾♂♀♃☿	20 Grad:	♍♐♑♋♏♌	Hora	☉☾♂♀♃☿
☿	♄♃☉♂♀☾☉	1 Grad:	♌♍♋♉♈♐♒	Hora.	♄♃☉♂♀☾☉
☾	☉♀♂♃♄☿	12 Grad:	♊♈♐♏♎♌	Hora.	☉♀♂♃♄☿
♂	☿♄♃♀☾☉	18 Grad:	♌♋♉♐♏♍	Hora.	☿♄♃♀☾☉
♃	☉☾♀♂♄☿	3 Grad:	♒♏♎♋♌	Hora.	☉☾♀♂♄☿
♀	☿♄♃☉♂☾☉	9 Grad:	♌♋♈♐♒♐	Hora.	☿♄♃☉♂☾☉

Table of the Conjunction and Transmutation of the Metals[22]

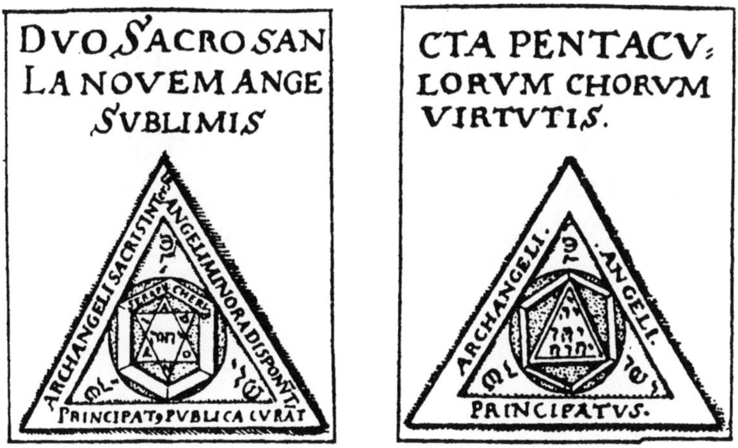

Two Sacrosanct Pentacles of the Nine Angelic Choirs
of Sublime Virtue[23]

ח	ד	א ·
SERAPHIM.	CHERVBIM.	THRONI
METATRON.	OPHANIEL.	ZAPHKIEL.
SAPHIRVS.	SMARAGDVS.	CARBV̄CVLVS.
PRIMV̄ MOBILE.	COEL: STELLAT:	SPHÆRA ♄
CALLIOPE.	VRANIA.	POLYMNIA.
MEMORIA.	COGITATIVA	IMAGINATIO.
CRIBRONIVS.	PICIONIVS.	AMPHIETVS.

NINE

The nine lettered Name of God: Tetragrammaton Sabaoth

	ה	ו	א
Nine Angelic Choirs	Seraphim	Cherubim	Thrones
Nine Angels Ruling Heaven	Metatron	Ophaniel	Zaphkiel
Nine Stones Representing the Angelic Choirs	Sapphire	Emerald	Ruby
Nine Moving Spheres	Primum Mobile	Heaven of the Fixed Stars	Sphere of Saturn
Nine Muses[24]	Calliope	Urania	Polyhymnia
Nine Interior and Exterior Senses	Memory	Thought	Imagination
Nine Bacchic Muses[25]	Cribronius	Picionius	Amphietus

The Nonary of the celestial spheres and of the divine spirits, assisting in order, sacred to the Muses.

ב	ע	ח
DOMINATIOn:	POTESTATES.	VIRTVTES.
ZADKIEL.	CAMAEL.	RAPHAEL.
BERILVS.	ONIX.	CRYSOLITVS.
SPHÆRA. ♃	SPHÆRA. ♂	SPHÆRA. ☉
TERPSICHO.	CLIO.	MELPOME.
SENSVS CON:	AVDITVS.	VISVS.
SABASIVS.	BASSARIVS.	TRIETENICVS.

NINE

	ב	צ	ה
Nine Angelic Choirs	Dominations	Powers	Virtues
Nine Angels Ruling Heaven	Zadkiel	Camael	Raphael
Nine Stones Representing the Angelic Choirs	Beryl	Onxy	Crystal
Nine Moving Spheres	Sphere of Jupiter	Sphere of Mars	Sphere of the Sun
Nine Muses[24]	Terpsichore	Clio	Melpomene
Nine Interior and Exterior Senses	Senses conjoined	Hearing	Vision
Nine Bacchic Muses[25]	Sabasius	Bassarius	Trietenicus

ז	ח	י
Principatvs.	Archangeli.	Angeli.
Haniel.	Michael.	Gabriel.
Iaspis.	Topasivs.	Sardivs.
Sphæra. ♀	Sphæra. ☿	Sphæra. ☽
Erato.	Evterpe.	Thalia.
Odoratvs.	Gvstvs.	Tactvs.
Lysivs.	Silenvs.	Lyævs.

NINE

	ו	ה	י
Nine Angelic Choirs	Principalities	Archangels	Angels
Nine Angels Ruling Heaven	Haniel	Michael	Gabriel
Nine Stones Representing the Angelic Choirs	Jasper	Topaz	Sardonyx
Nine Moving Spheres	Sphere of Venus	Sphere of Mercury	Sphere of the Moon
Nine Muses[24]	Erato	Euterpe	Thalia
Nine Interior and Exterior Senses	Smell	Taste	Touch
Nine Bacchic Muses[25]	Lysius	Silenus	Lyaeus

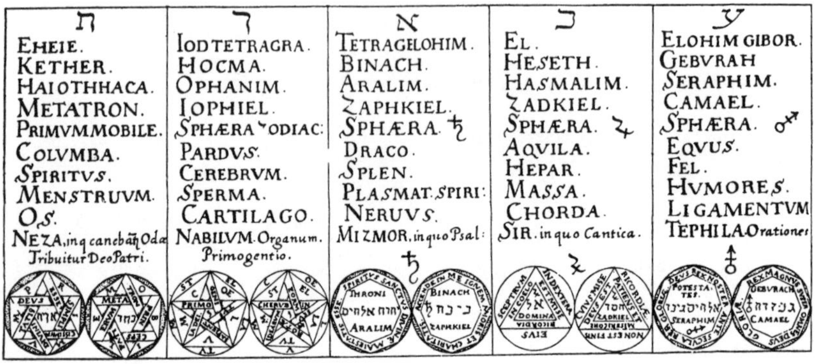
ה
EHEIE.
KETHER.
HAIOTHHACA.
METATRON.
PRIMVMMOBILE.
COLVMBA.
SPIRITVS.
MENSTRUVM.
OS.
NEZA, in q canebāt Odæ Tribuitur Deo Patri.
י
IODTETRAGRA.
HOCMA.
OPHANIM.
IOPHIEL.
SPHÆRA ZODIAC:
PARDVS.
CEREBRVM.
SPERMA.
CARTILAGO.
NABILVM. Organum. Primogentio.
א
TETRAGELOHIM.
BINACH.
ARALIM.
ZAPHKIEL.
SPHÆRA. ♄
DRACO.
SPLEN.
PLASMAT. SPIRI:
NERUVS.
MIZMOR. in quo Psal:
ב
EL.
HESETH.
HASMALIM.
ZADKIEL.
SPHÆRA. ♃
AQVILA.
HEPAR.
MASSA.
CHORDA.
SIR. in quo Cantica.
ע
ELOHIM GIBOR.
GEBVRAH
SERAPHIM.
CAMAEL.
SPHÆRA. ♂
EQVUS.
FEL.
HVMORES.
LIGAMENTVM
TEPHILA. Orationes

The ten lettered Name of God: Elohim Sabaoth

	ה	ו	א	ב	צ
Ten Names of God	Eheie	Iod Tetragrammaton	Tetragrammaton Elohim	El Heseth	Elohim Gibor
Ten Sephiroth	Kether	Chokmah	Binah	Chesed	Geburah
Ten Orders of the Blessed	Haiothhaca	Ophanim	Aralim	Hasmalim	Seraphim
Ten Archangels	Metatron	Iophiel	Zaphkiel	Zadkiel	Camael
Ten Heavenly Spheres	Primum Mobile	Zodiacal Sphere	Sphere of Saturn	Sphere of Jupiter	Sphere of Mars
Ten Sacred Animals	Dove	Leopard	Dragon	Eagle	Horse
Ten Organs Inside Man	Spirit	Brain	Spleen	Liver	Gall
Ten Parts of the Blood of Man	Menstruum	Sperm	Plasma	Clot	Humors
Ten Tissues of Man	Bone	Cartilage	Nerves	Gut	Ligament
Ten Musical Instruments	Neza, to which were sung the Odes to God the Father	Nabilum, the organ of the first peoples	Mizmor, to which Psalms were sung	Sir Canticles	Tephila Orations
Spheres	[Primum Mobile]	[Heaven of the Stars]	♄	♃	♂

The Denary—The end and fulfillment of the Numbers—of many powers, a perfect number.

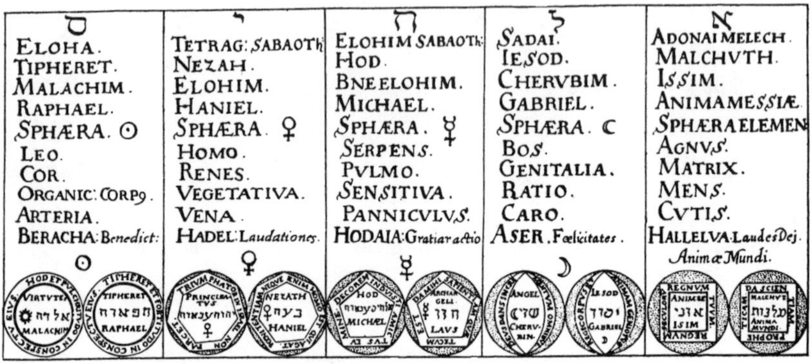
ט
ELOHA.
TIPHERET.
MALACHIM.
RAPHAEL.
SPHÆRA. ☉
LEO.
COR.
ORGANIC: CORP9.
ARTERIA.
BERACHA: Benedict:
☉
י
TETRAG: SABAOTH
NEZAH.
ELOHIM.
HANIEL.
SPHÆRA. ♀
HOMO.
RENES.
VEGETATIVA.
VENA.
HADEL: Laudationes.
♀
ח
ELOHIM SABAOTH.
HOD.
BNEELOHIM.
MICHAEL.
SPHÆRA. ☿
SERPENS.
PVLMO.
SENSITIVA.
PANNICVLVS.
HODAIA: Gratiar actio
☿
ל
SADAI.
IESOD.
CHERVBIM.
GABRIEL.
SPHÆRA. ☾
BOS.
GENITALIA.
RATIO.
CARO.
ASER. Fœlicitates.
☽
א
ADONAI MELECH.
MALCHVTH.
ISSIM.
ANIMAMESSIÆ.
SPHÆRA ELEMEN
AGNVS.
MATRIX.
MENS.
CVTIS.
HALLELVA: Laudes Dei.
Animæ Mundi.

	מ	י	ה	ל	א
Ten Names of God	Eloha	Tetragramm-aton Sabaoth	Elohim Sabaoth	Sadai	Adonai Melech
Ten Sephiroth	Tiphereth	Netzach	Hod	Yesod	Malkuth
Ten Orders of the Blessed	Malachim	Elohim	Bene Elohim	Cherubim	Issim
Ten Archangels	Raphael	Haniel	Michael	Gabriel	Soul of the Messiah
Ten Heavenly Spheres	Sphere of the Sun	Sphere of Venus	Sphere of Mercury	Sphere of Moon	Sphere of Elements
Ten Sacred Animals	Lion	Man	Snake	Cow	Lamb
Ten Organs Inside Man	Heart	Kidneys	Lungs	Genitals	Womb
Ten Parts of the Blood of Man	Organic body	Life force	Sensation	Reason	Mind
Ten Tissues of Man	Arteries	Veins	Membrane	Flesh	Skin
Ten Musical Instruments	Beracha Benedictions	Hadel Praises	Hodaia Thanks-givings	Aser Felicities	Hallelujah Praising God
Spheres	☉	♀	☿	☽	Soul of the World

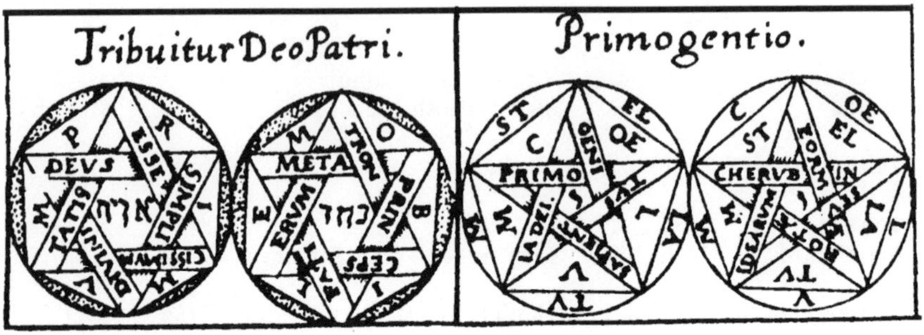
Tribuitur Deo Patri.
Primogentio.
DEVS
META
PRIMO
CHERVB

26

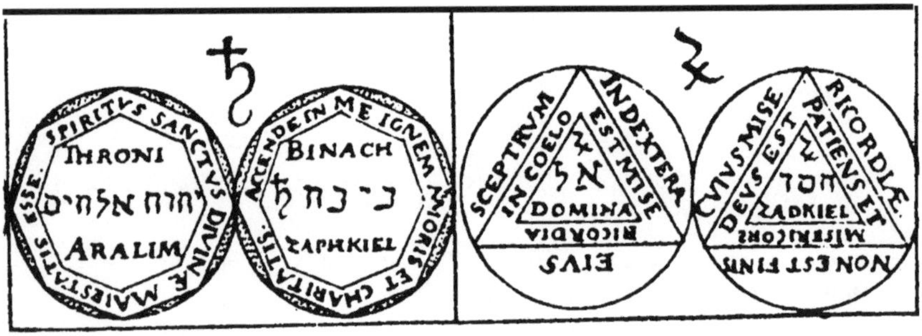
SPIRITVS SANCTVS DIVINAE MAIESTATIS ESSE
THRONI
יהוה אלהים
ARALIM
ACCENDE IN ME IGNEM AMORIS ET CHARITATIS
BINACH
ZAPHKIEL
SCEPTRVM IN COELO
IN DEXTERA EST MISE
RICORDIA
EIVS
DOMINA
CVIVS MISE RICORDIAE
DEVS EST PATIENS ET
ZADKIEL
NON EST FINIS

TEN

DEVS REX NOSTER ANTE SECVLA REX GLORIÆ
POTESTATES
SERAPHIM
REX MAGNVS SVPER OMNES DEVS GLORIÆ
GEBVRACH
CAMAEL
HOD ET PVLCHRITVDO IN CONSPECTV EIVS
VIRTVTES
MALACHIM
TIPHERET ET FORTITVDO IN CONSPECTV EIVS
TIPHERET
RAPHAEL

26

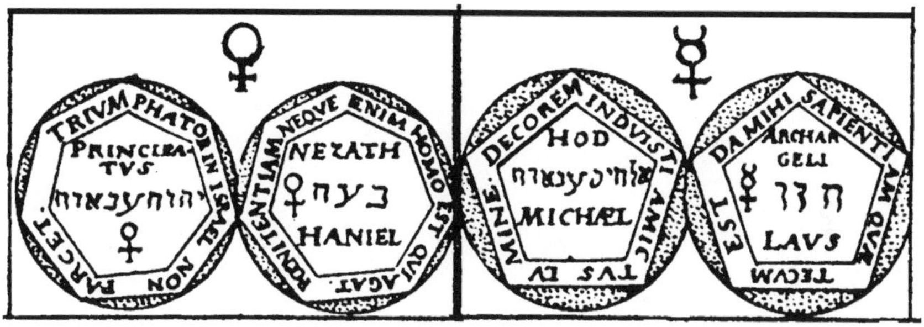
TRIVMPHATOR IN ISRAEL NON PARCET
PRINCIPATVS
NEQVE ENIM HOMO EST QVI AGAT POENITENTIAM
NEZATH
HANIEL
DECOREM INDVISTI AMICTVS LVMINE
HOD
MICHAEL
DA MIHI SAPIENTIAM QVAE TECVM EST
ARCHANGELI
LAVS

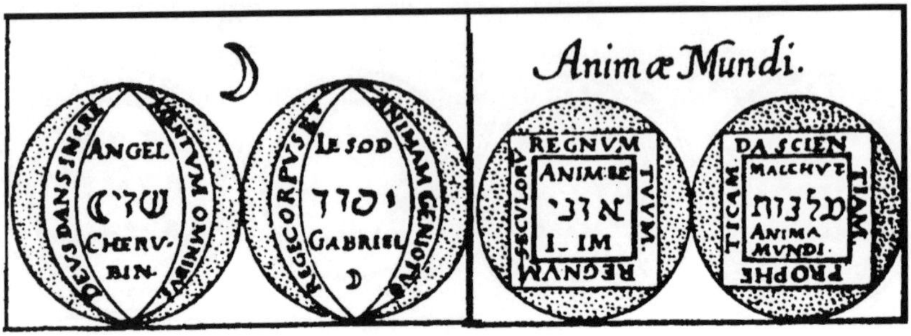
Animæ Mundi.
ANGEL
שדי
CHERV-
BIN.
LESOD
יסוד
GABRIEL
REGNVM
TVVM.
REGNVM
DA SCIEN
TIAM.
TICAM
PROPHE
MALCHVT
מלכות
ANIMA
MVNDI.

26

ELEVEN

The Undenary has not any merit, just as it exceeds the Denary, which is of law and order, so it falls short of the Duodenary, which is grace and perfection: therefore this number is said to be that of sinners and penances.

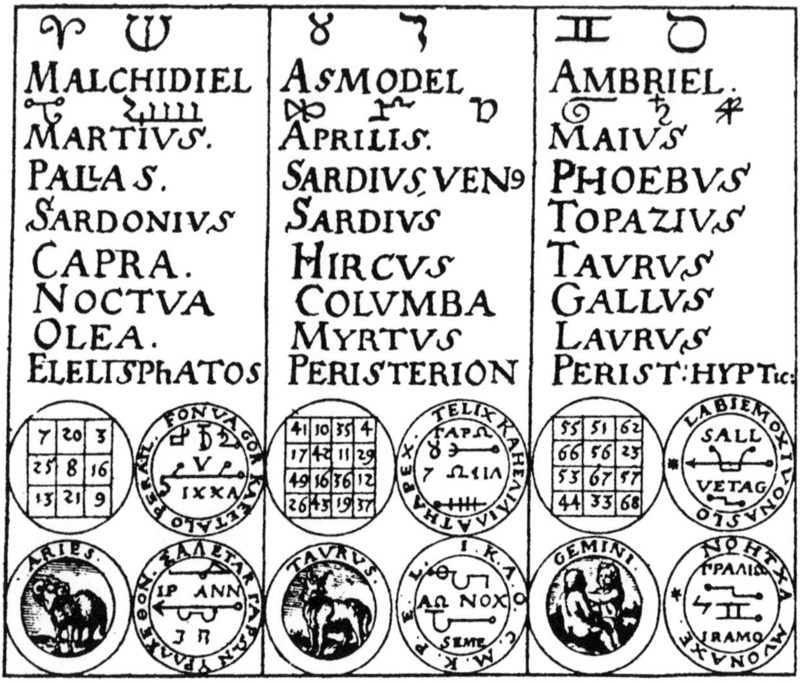

♈ ♅	♉ ♼	♊ ☽
MALCHIDIEL	ASMODEL	AMBRIEL
MARTIVS.	APRILIS.	MAIVS
PALLAS.	SARDIVS, VEN⁹	PHOEBVS
SARDONIVS	SARDIVS	TOPAZIVS
CAPRA.	HIRCVS	TAVRVS
NOCTVA	COLVMBA	GALLVS
OLEA.	MYRTVS	LAVRVS
ELELISPHATOS	PERISTERION	PERIST: HYPTᴵᶜ:

29 30

The twelve lettered Name of God: Father, Son and Holy Spirit[27]

	ש	ד	ק
Twelve Angels of the Signs with Characters[28]	Malchidiel	Asmodel	Ambriel
Twelve Months	March	April	May
Twelve Divinities	Pallas	Venus of Sardis	Phoebus
Twelve Stones	Sardonyx	Sard	Topaz
Twelve Animals	She goat	Billy goat	Bull
Twelve Sacred Birds	Owl	Dove	Cock
Twelve Sacred Trees	Olive	Myrtle	Laurel
Twelve Sacred Plants	Sage	Upright Vervain	Bending Vervain

The Duodenary, the number of the Celestial Signs, is the pre-eminent means for the support of spirits

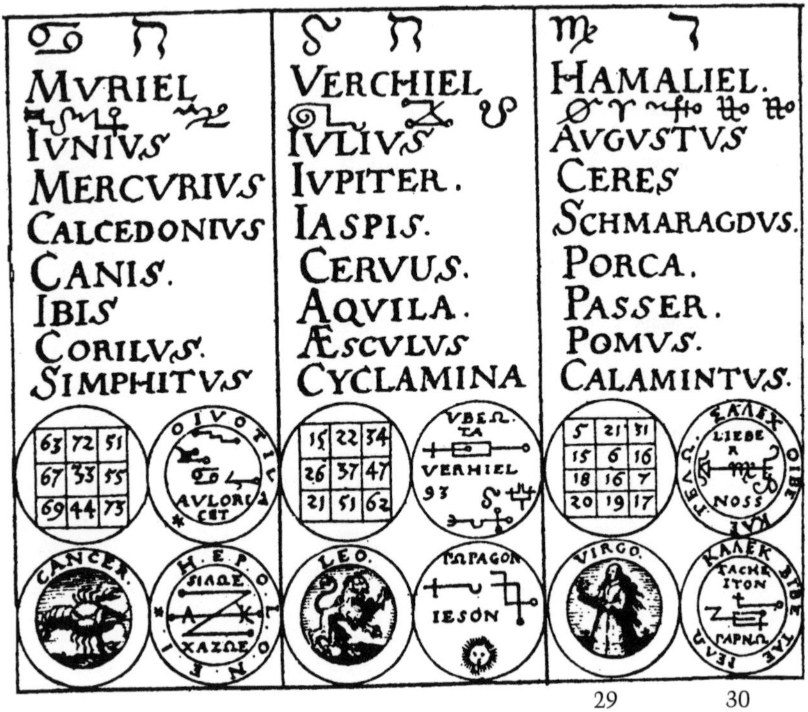
MVRIEL
IVNIVS
MERCVRIVS
CALCEDONIVS
CANIS.
IBIS
CORILVS.
SIMPHITVS
VERCHIEL
IVLIVS
IVPITER.
IASPIS.
CERVUS.
AQVILA.
ÆSCVLVS
CYCLAMINA
HAMALIEL.
AVGVSTVS
CERES
SCHMARAGDVS.
PORCA.
PASSER.
POMVS.
CALAMINTVS.
VERHIEL
CANCER
LEO
IESON
VIRGO
LIEBE
NOSS

29 30

	ה	ח	ו
Twelve Angels of the Signs with Characters[28]	Muriel	Verchiel	Hamaliel
Twelve Months	June	July	August
Twelve Divinities	Mercury	Jupiter	Ceres
Twelve Stones	Chalcedony	Jasper	Emerald
Twelve Animals	Dog	Stag	Pig
Twelve Sacred Birds	Ibis	Eagle	Sparrow
Twelve Sacred Trees	Hazel	Chestnut	Pear
Twelve Sacred Plants	Comfrey	Cyclamen	Calamint

ZVRIEL.
SEPTEMBER.
VVLCANVS.
BERILLVS.
ASINVS.
ANSER.
BVXVS.
SCORIVROS.
BARBIEL.
OCTOBER.
MARS.
AMETHISTVS.
LVPVS.
PICVS.
CORNVS.
ARTEMISIA.
ADNACHIEL.
NOVEMBER.
DIANA.
HYACINTHVS.
CERVA.
CORNIX.
PALMA.
ANAGALLIS.
LIBRA.
SCORPIO.
SAGITARIVS.

29 30

	ר	ו	ז
Twelve Angels of the Signs with Characters[28]	Zuriel	Barbiel	Adnachiel
Twelve Months	September	October	November
Twelve Divinities	Vulcan	Mars	Diana
Twelve Stones	Beryl	Amethyst	Jacinth
Twelve Animals	Ass	Wolf	Deer
Twelve Sacred Birds	Goose	Woodpecker	Crow
Twelve Sacred Trees	Box	Dogwood	Palm
Twelve Sacred Plants	Garlic	Wormwood	Pimpernel

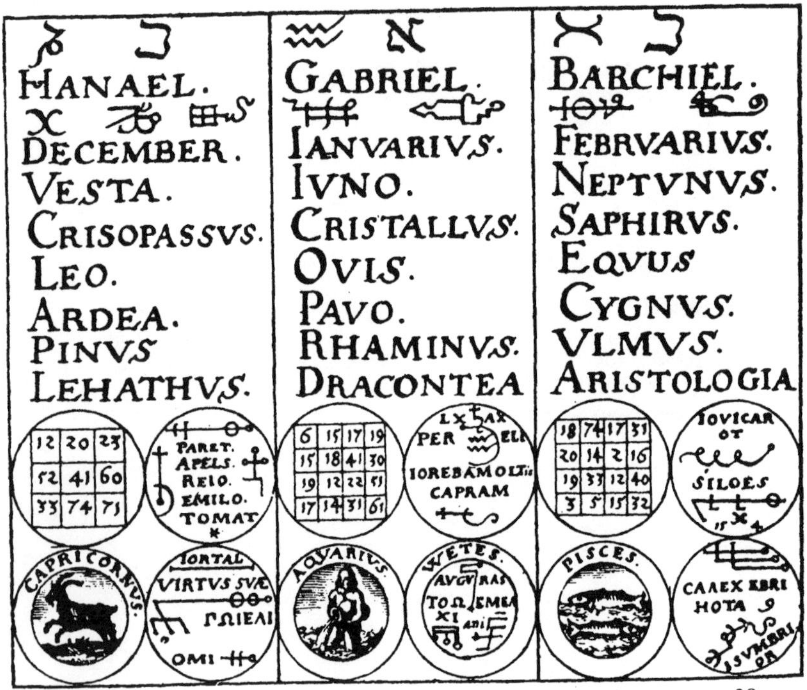
HANAEL.
DECEMBER.
VESTA.
CRISOPASSVS.
LEO.
ARDEA.
PINVS
LEHATHVS.
GABRIEL.
IANVARIVS.
IVNO.
CRISTALLVS.
OVIS.
PAVO.
RHAMINVS.
DRACONTEA
BARCHIEL.
FEBRVARIVS.
NEPTVNVS.
SAPHIRVS.
EQVUS
CYGNVS.
VLMVS.
ARISTOLOGIA
CAPRICORNVS.
VIRTVS SVÆ
AQVARIVS
PISCES.
SILOES

29 30

	ב	ב	א
Twelve Angels of the Signs with Characters[28]	Hanael	Gabriel	Barchiel
Twelve Months	December	January	February
Twelve Divinities	Vesta	Juno	Neptune
Twelve Stones	Chrisophrase	Crystal	Sapphire
Twelve Animals	Lion	Sheep	Horse
Twelve Sacred Birds	Heron	Peacock	Swan
Twelve Sacred Trees	Pine	Buckthorn	Elm
Twelve Sacred Plants	Dock	Dragonwort	Birthwort

Notes and Commentary

1. These symbols are derived from the geomantic figures for the Dragon's Head ☊ and the Dragon's Tail ☋, the ascending and descending nodes of the Moon.

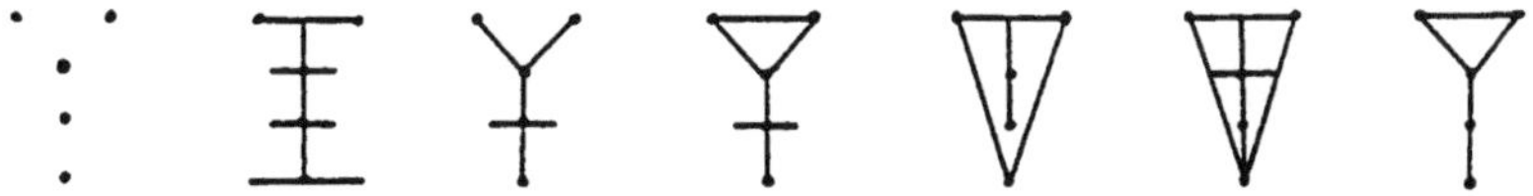

Dragon's
Head

Dragon's
Tail

2. In this group of twelve symbols, God the Father, Adonai, is associated with the hexagram ✡, the interlaced triangles, and is shown as an old crowned king. The Resurrected Christ is shown against a five pointed star, and we see the Holy Spirit as a dove in a nimbus of light. On the top fourth symbol it is indicated that Christ is supported by Jehovah and does not move from his right hand.

The Christ is associated with the pentagram ★, and in particular with the transformation of the Tetragammaton into the five lettered name, Jesus. We also have a reference to "the lion of the tribe of Judea conquers," and the famous "paternoster" acrostic:

S A T O R
A R E P O
T E N E T
O P E R A
R O T A S

The Holy Spirit is indicated as proceeding from the Father and the Son, and is associated with the fourfold and the threefold.

3. We have here the names of the four Elements in Hebrew:

Fire	אש	Water	מים
Air	רוח	Earth	עפר

4. The four Archangels are mentioned in *1 Enoch* chapter 20.

Raphael	- "the healing of God"	- set over the diseases and wounds of Man
Michael	- "like unto God"	- set over the bodies of Man
Gabriel	- "mighty one of God"	- set over Paradise
Uriel	- "the light of God"	- set over the world and Tartarus.

5. We have here an unusual set of symbols for the elements, the more familiar ones being shown in the second column below. In the third column are a related set of symbols from the *Sworn Book of Honorius*.

Fire	△	△	△
Air	#	🜁	○
Water	▽	▽	▽
Earth	⊖	🜃	□

The familiar symbols are rather abstract in form and are derived from the two interlaced triangles ✡. The other group are perhaps more suited to giving an imaginative picture of the elements. △ Fire and ▽ Water are opposites; Fire always rises upwards, Water always seeks the lowest point. Air in its circulatory nature is well pictured by ○, and the stable solidity of Earth by □. The opposite natures of the Earth and Air elements are well pictured by the opposing qualities of the circle and the square.

6. These names of the four Seasons, the Angels of the four Seasons, their Rulers, and the four names of the Earth, are found in both the *Heptameron* of Peter of Abano (1250–1317), and the *Sworn Book of Honorius* (possibly thirteenth century, but more likely dating to the fifteenth century).

The engraver of the *Magical Calendar* made an error in attributing these names, muddling Gaviel and Tubiel, which he had corrected on the plate using the superscripts [1] and [2] to indicate the correct order.

	Spring	Summer	Autumn	Winter
Four Rulers of the Sun	Abraym	Athemay	Abragini	Commutaf
Four Rulers of the Moon	Agusta	Armatas	Matasignais	Affaterim

7. From the *Goetia* or *Lesser Key of Solomon*:

Baell - "The first principal spirit is a King ruling in the East. He makes men invisible and rules over 66 legions of inferior spirits. He appears in diverse forms and sometimes in various forms at once."

Paimon - "A great King, very obedient to Lucifer, teaches all arts and sciences. He is observed towards the North-West, and is of the Order of Dominions."

8. Although these names for the elementary spirits are found in the writings of Paracelsus, the more usual names are:

Fire	Salamanders
Air	Sylphs
Water	Nymphs or Undines
Earth	Gnomes

9. The "Seven Gifts" seem to have been rather garbled by the compiler or misplaced by the engraver. Perhaps the true arrangement, taking note of the traditional qualities of the planets, should be as follows:

♄	Spirit of Wisdom
♃	Spirit of Judgement
♂	Spirit of Courage
☉	Spirit of Intelligence
♀	Spirit of Affection
☿	Spirit of Science
☽	Spirit of Fear

10. The source of these characters of the seven Olympian Spirits is the *Arbatel of Magick*, first published in Latin in 1575, and later (1655) included in Robert Turner's translation of the *Fourth Book of Occult Philosophy* (which is erroneously ascribed to Agrippa). The *Arbatel* indicates that the Olympian Spirits inhabit the firmament, are of an elevated spiritual nature, and cannot be invoked but for divine purposes. They rule through lower provinces of subordinate spirits, and this reveals a further seven-fold structure:

Aratron rules	49	provinces
Bethor	42	
Phaleg	35	
Och	28	
Hagith	21	
Ophiel	14	
Phul	7	

The *Arbatel* goes on to describe in some detail the realms of activity of these spirits and gives some indications upon the use of the characters.

11. The Archangels and their sigils associated with the planets have here been rather muddled. In particular, Raphael, Michael and Anael are confused. The proper arrangement is:

♄	Casiel	
♃	Sachiel	
♂	Samael	
☉	Michael	
♀	Anael	
☿	Raphael	
☽	Gabriel	

Though we can put this down to an engraver's mistake, perhaps even an intentional confusion, there is an occult reality behind the interchange of Michael and Raphael as Archangels of the Sun and Mercury. Many sources from the 16th and 17th centuries assign these two Archangelic planetary guardians differently. Trithemius associated these seven Archangels with a seven-fold historical cycle, which can be approximately correlated with the Platonic Age of 2,160 years, the time taken for the Sun to precess through one sign of the Zodiac. Each Archangel acted in turn as a Spirit of the Epoch for a part of this Platonic cycle of 2,160 years, lasting approximately 350 years, and it is possible that, from this tradition, that the confusion arose. Thus, according to one method of computation, the age of Michael began in 1879, and the previous age of Gabriel began in the mid-sixteenth century. It may be that during this transition age of the mid-sixteenth century, two distinct traditions arose about the Archangelic rulership of the epochs.

12. The fact that we have here four sets of sigils associated with the seven planets might lead us to inquire as to their esoteric significance. These can be correlated with the four Worlds of the Kabbalah:

Atziluth	World of Emanation	Seven Angels of the Presence
Briah	World of Creation	Olympian Spirits
Yetzirah	World of Formation	Planetary Angels
Assiah	World of Matter	Planets

Thus the sigils are symbol-keys that open us to awareness on that particular plane or realm of being. They should be used in ritual or meditative work, together with other symbols and structures relating to these levels. Therefore, awareness of the plane to which a sigil relates, is essential to understanding its function and its use as a symbol-key.

From another perspective, it is interesting to note that if we also include the Sigils of the Planets, the Characters of the Planets, and the Divine Letters, then for the seven-fold we have a total of seven sets of sigils.

13. These symbols are derived from the Geomantic figure associated with the planets, as found in Agrippa.

♄
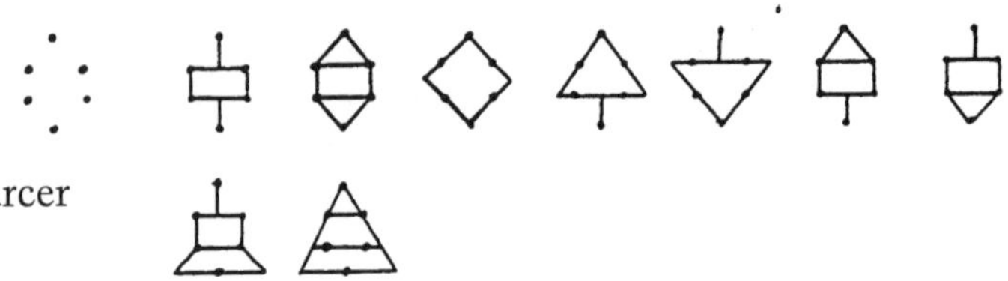
Carcer

♄

Tristitia

♃  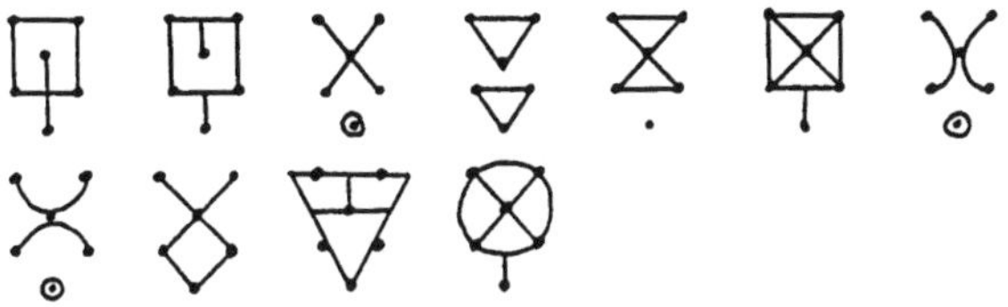

Acquisito

♃ 

Laetitia
[This figure does not seem to be represented in this series]

♂  

Rubeus

♂  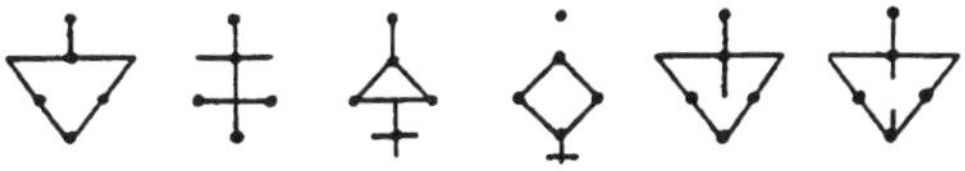

Puer

☉ 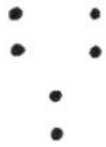 

Greater Fortune

☉  

Lesser Fortune

♀  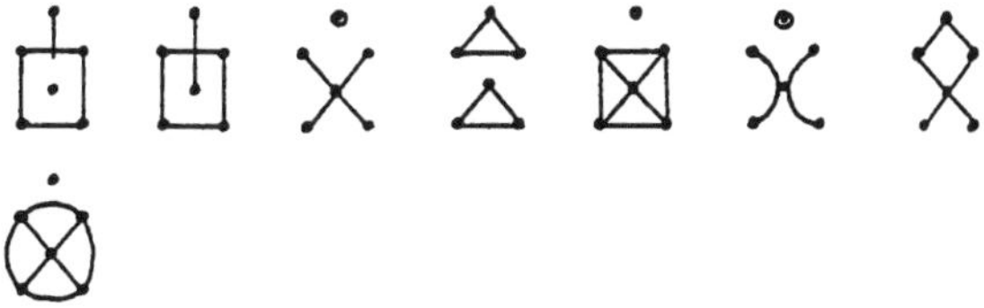

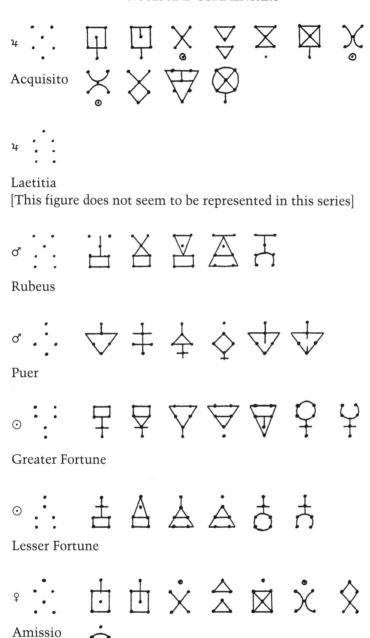

Amissio

♀ 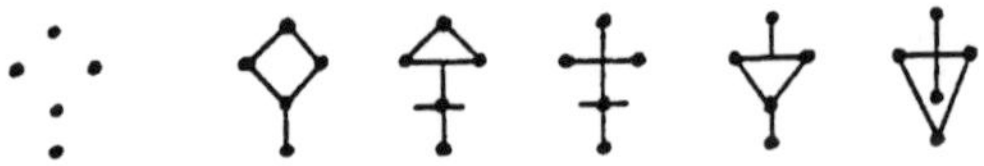

Puella

☿ 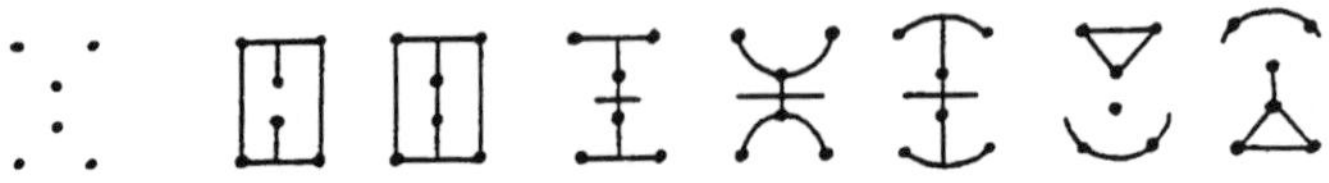

Coniunctio 

☿ 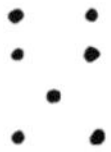

Albus
[This figure does not seem to be represented in this series]

☽ 

Via

☽ 

Populus

14. Onomancy is the method of divination from the letters of a name. These seven Onomantic Tables of the Planets predict in the world of the elements, health, fortune, life and death. Although these Onomantic tables will be of little use to the serious occultist seeking the spirit behind esoteric facts, I include for the sake of completeness a description of the use of this system of fortune telling found in the *Magical Calendar* manuscript probably made by Sigismund Bacstrom (MS. Ferguson 2). This section is approximately 15 pages of Latin text.

Table of Albumasar for Saturn

As each letter of the alphabet appears in this table of Albumasar, it has a number, as also does each day of the week. Therefore, if Antonio wishes to know if perhaps the day of Mars was lucky or unlucky, assuming his baptismal name is Antonius, and writing it in the nominative case in Latin, then the particular numbers of the individual letters, and also the number of the day of Mars, and that of the age of the Moon, is computed, then the total is divided by 30, and the remainder by division will give the reply to the question asked, as is seen in the following example:

A	N	T	O	N	I	U	S		
3	22	18	11	22	15	4	20	The sum total of Antonius	98
								The day of Mars	12
								The age of the Moon	23
									133

130 divided by 30, leaves a remainder of 13, which is found in the column of Life (Vita) of the above table, and it is signified that the day of Mars was lucky and auspicious for Antonius, and whenever the number is found in a different column, other things are signified.

Table of Pythagoras for Jupiter

The pattern of this table, is to take the name of the person, just as in the above described table of Albumasar, and to compute its numbers with that of the age of the Moon, and divide by the number 29. When the number remaining is found in the column of life, it is good and happens easily; if the number is in the column of medium, the things happen with difficulties; in the column of hope, it is good but endures too little, and so for the rest. Peter is to know whether it will be fortunate or unfortunate, if he departs from Paris for a second time to the war against the Germans, on the day of the Moon in the month of March, in the year 1734.

P	E	T	R	U	S		
4	15	18	13	6	20	The sum total of Petrus	76
						The age of the Moon	25
							101

101 divided by 29, the remainder is 14, which is found in the column of life, and this signifies this departure of Peter is fortunate, and he will not die in the war; but if the number remaining is 4, 5, 8 or 9, which are found in the column of Death, then the departure is unfortunate and death is signified in the war.

Table of Ptolemy for Mars

The pattern of this table is the same as that of Pythagoras, with it however different in that the number of the name of the person and days, is divided by 30. Consequently, if they wish to know whether the day of Mars is fortunate or unfortunate for Peter, it is seen in the example following.

P E T R U S

The sum total of Petrus	83
Day of Mars	70
	153

The number 153 divided by 30 remains, which is found in the table of Ptolemy beneath the column of middle life, which signifies to be resolved with difficulty. When it is done concerning some illness, the number of his age, and of his name, and also the number of the day on which the illness, are taken up.

Petrus, 49 years of age, began to be ill on the day of Mars. It is to be known, whether he will live or die.

P E T R U S

The sum total of Petrus	83
Age	49
Day of Mars	70
	202

This number 202 divided by 30 the remaining number is 22, which in the Ptolemaic table is denoted a favourable outcome.

Table of Anthidonis for the Sun

The pattern of this table is the same as that of Albumasar, with the difference that the number of the total is divided by 30 in that table, while in this table it is divided by 29. It is shown in the following example which was to find whether the day of Mars was lucky or unlucky for Antonio.

A N T O N I U S

The sum total of Antonius	113
Day of Mars	2
The age of the Moon	23
	138

Which number being divided by 29 as has already been described, the remaining number is 22, which is found in the column of Life, which indicates that the day of Mars may be fortunate for Antonio. When the remaining number is found in the middle life, it foretells indifferent fortune, and when in the column Dubium, short lived fortune is promised. When the same remaining number is in the column of Death, great ill fortune or death, and when the number is found in the column of ill fortune of this table, illness, loss, and bad luck is denoted, and all evil is foretold.

Table of Plato for Venus

"The pattern of this table is the same for that of Pythagoras, and the number of the person's name, of the day which it was questioned about, and the age of the Moon, and the sum is divided by 30, of which division is devoted to the knowing of the good or evil fortune which the man is having in regard to business, in journeys, in combat, in law suits, in love-making, or in anything different. When the question is concerning some illness, take the number of the person's name, and the day on which the illness seized hold. When they wish to know who will die first, whether the husband or the wife, divide both names by 7. If it will be done concerning two simultaneous certainties, divide both name separately by 9. For knowing which of two horses will be faster in running a race, the number of the day on which they should race is taken, and the numbers of the letters in the names of the colours of both horses, and divide them separately by 30. If the number remaining, made by division, is found in the column of life in this table, life, profit, joy and good is promised anyhow, and the opposite in the column of death; and thus concerning the others.

Table of Aristotle for Mercury

When you wish to know which will be the first to die, whether the husband or the wife, or which of two possibilities will prevail, and in another way of which method to use, take the numbers of the names of the persons, and the day on which it was questioned, and divide these separately by 7. If you are to know whether he will die of an illness or not, divide the number of the name of the person, and the number of the day on which the illness began, separately by 9.

Antonius is ill on the Lord's day: it is to be known whether he shall die or not.

Antonius 83, which number divided by 9, the remainder is 2.

The Lord's Day, which number divided by 9, the remainder is 6.

Therefore, there is of the remaining numbers 2 against 6, and indeed it appears in the following table, for 2 against 6, 2 overcomes, which suggests that Antonio will not die.

If you wish to know good or bad fortune on a journey, or for trade, divide the numbers of the person and day separately by 9. If you are to know which of two overcomes when they play together any kind of game, take the number of the first person and the number of the day on which they sport, and these two numbers divide by 9 separately, then take the number of the second person and the day, and equally they are divided separately by 9, and from the numbers which remain from both divisions, the answer is had, as appears in the following example.

Antonius and Petrus play together on the Lord's day. It is to be known which of these will win.

A N T O N I U S		83
	The Lord's Day	24
		107

Which number divided by 9, the remainder is 8.

P E T R U S		73
	The Lord's Day	24
		97

Which number divided by 9, the remainder is 7.
So "7 against 8," and according to the following table "8" overcomes, therefore Antonius having in his division "8," he wins.
In this table of the talented Aristotle, the answers are discovered to whatever questions and whatever uncertain requests.

TABULA RESPONSIONŨ

1. Contra 1. Minor Vincet.	2. Contre 3. 3. Vincet.
1. contra 2. 2...... Vincet	2. contre 4. 2. Vincet.
1. Contra 3. 1...... Vincet	2. Contre 5. 5. Vincet.
1. contra 4. 4...... Vincet	2. Contre 6. 2. Vincet
1. Contra 5. 1...... Vincet	2. Contre 7. 7. Vincet
1. Contra 6. 6...... Vincet	2. Contre 8. 2. Vincet
1. Contra 7. 1..... Vincet	2. Contre 9. 9. Vincet
1. Contra 8. 8..... Vincet	3. Contre 3. Minor Vincet.
1. Contra 9. 1..... Vincet	3. contre 4. 4.... Vincet.
2. Contra 2. Major Vincet	3. contre 5. 3..... Vincet.
3. contra 6. 6... Vincet	5. Contra 8. 8. Vincet.
3. contra 7. 3.... Vincet.	5. contra 9. 5... Vincet.
3. Contra 8. 8..... Vincet.	6. contra 6 Major Vincet.
3. contra 9. 3..... Vincet.	6. contra 7. 7. Vincet
4. contra 4. Major Vincet	6. Contra 8. 6.... Vincet
4. contra 5. 5. ... Vincet	6. Contra 9. 9. Vincet.
4. contra 6. 4. ... Vincet	7. Contra 7. Minor Vincet.
4. contra 7. 7. ... Vincet	7. contra 8. 8.... Vincet.
4. contra 8. 4. ... Vincet	7. contra 9. 7. ... Vincet.
4. contra 9. 9. .... Vincet	8. contra 8. Major. Vincet
5. contra 5. Minor Vincet	8. Contra 9. 9. .... Vincet.
5. contra 6. 6..... Vincet	9. Contra 9. Minor Vincet.
5. contra 7. 5.... Vincet	

Table of Hali for the Moon

The pattern of this seventh and last table for the Moon and the philosopher Hali, is the same as the former of Aristotle which precedes. Therefore, according as you will know which of two rivals overcome between themselves, take the number of the name of one person and the number of the day on which they compete, and this same number should be divided by 9, then take the number of the name of the other person and the day, and divide similarly and separately these numbers by 9, and from the numbers produced by both divisions, you will have the answers from the table of Aristotle, in which you will see a similar example, and the pattern is as the other questions of whatever kind, between two persons or two animals.

Although it is easy to dismiss these Onomantic Tables as naive fortune telling devices, perhaps they serve to point us to the basic spiritual reality of the rhythmic patterns underlying human life. These have been recognized in recent years as "biorhythms," the regular cycles of energy in the human etheric body. The method of these tables presupposes repeating patterns of 29 and 30 days, which are in turn broken down into smaller units, to which the prognostications "lucky," "unlucky," etc., are applied.

15. When seen as a whole, the series of seven sigils within the polygons associated with the planets seem to be a metamorphosis of a basic form, which moves from an initial unity and connectedness, through gradually unfolding stages, to be ultimately resolved into two disconnected figures.

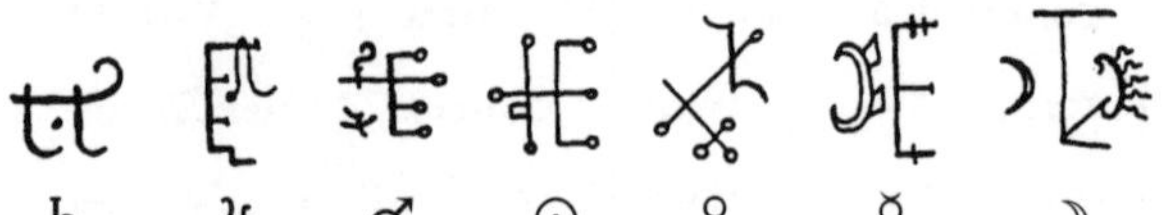

16. Athanasius Kircher includes in his *Oedipus Aegypticus* of 1652, some interesting illustrations which carry the magic square symbols further, enclosing each of the seven squares within a polygon with the appropriate number of sides. There are also some

interesting sigils which do not seem to be found elsewhere. Although this was published some thirty years after the *Magical Calendar,* it shows us a further development of these magical ideas. It is interesting that Kircher, a Jesuit, had the freedom within the Church establishment to pursue his philosophical and esoteric interests, and indeed to publish such material, which in an earlier age might have been thought heretical. We are reminded of the freedom which James Hepburn, the Keeper of the Oriental Books and Manuscripts at the Vatican at the beginning of the seventeenth century, seemed also to have to study and publish material on magical alphabets and the Kabbalah.

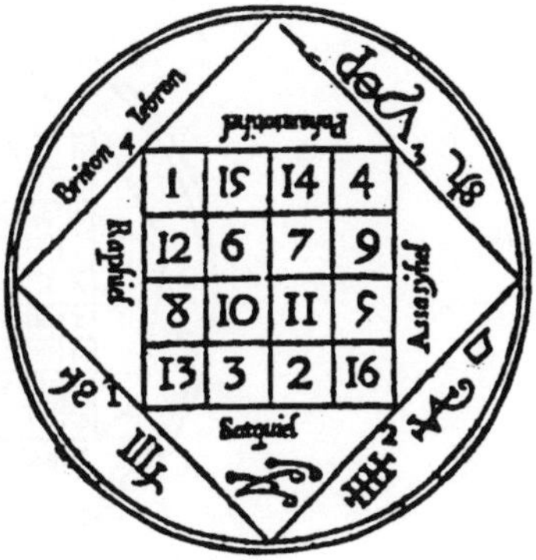

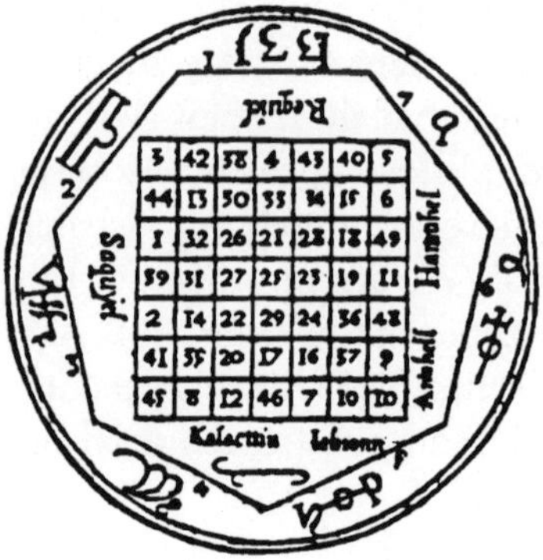

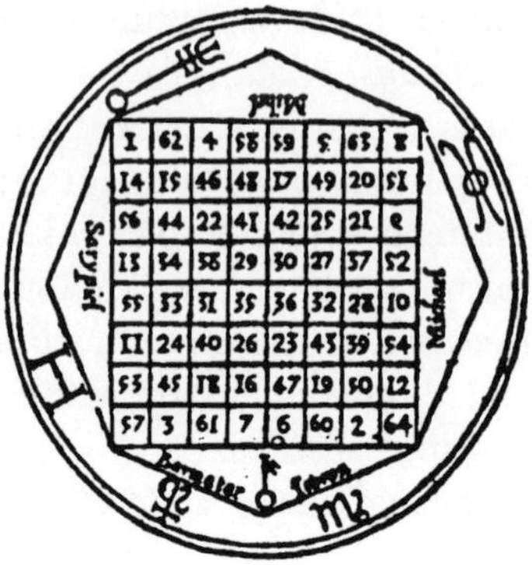
Michael

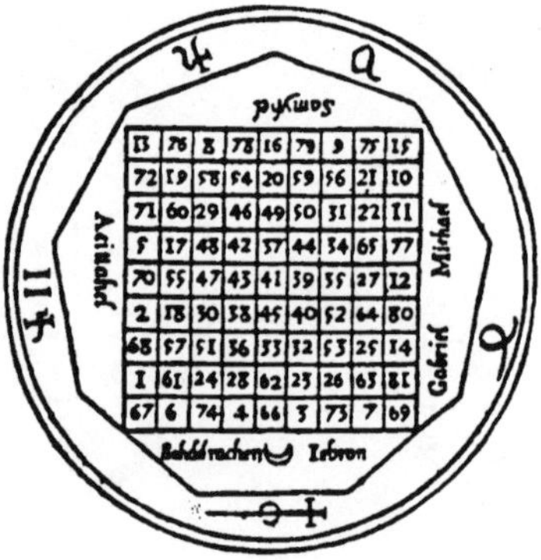
Michael
Gabriel
Iebron

17. The Kamea or Magical Squares of the planets can be used for constructing the pairs of sigils (those of the Intelligences and those of the Spirits of the seven planets), which are found in the outer ring of the Seal of each planet. On the *Magical Calendar* engraving, the space provided for these is so cramped, that the forms of these sigils have been rather corrupted, but they are essentially the same as those found in the *Three Books of Occult Philosophy* of Henry Cornelius Agrippa. Each sigil, as is shown below, can be derived from the name of the Intelligence or Spirit of the planet, by breaking it down into a pattern of numbers through kabbalistic reduction, and establishing this pattern on the magic square. These names are connected with the magic squares, being either the sum of a line, or the total of the whole square (with, in the case of Venus, the number of letters in the square). In general, this arrangement does not distinguish between units, tens and hundreds; i.e., 3, 30 or 300 can be represented by the single digit 3. On the following pages, the Intelligences are shown on the left and the Spirits on the right.

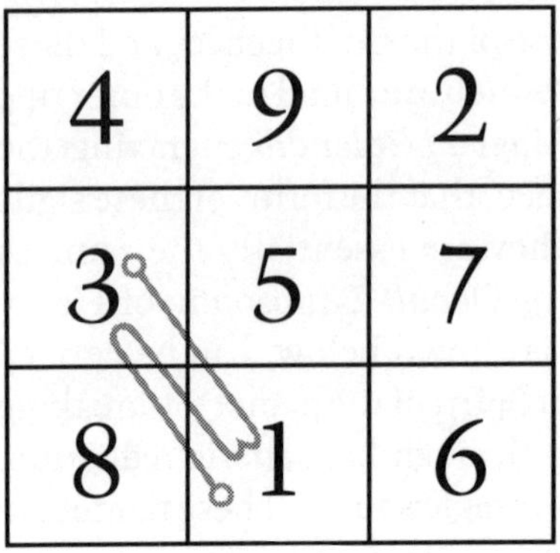

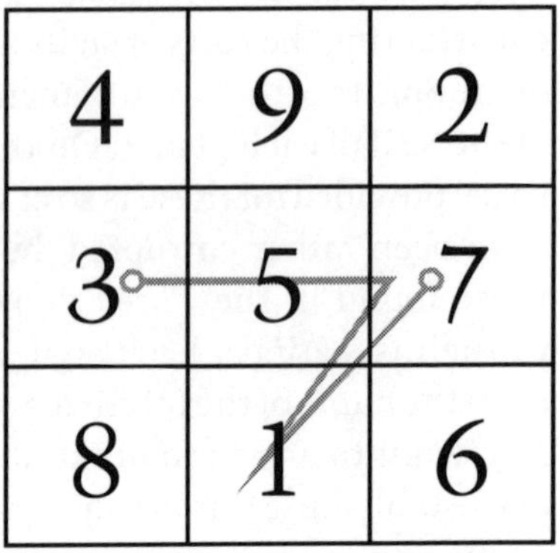

♄
Saturn

Saturn 3x3 **Sum along line 15** **Total 45**

AGIEL
אגיאל

30
1
10
3
1
45

ZAZEL
זאזל

30
7
1
7
45

4	14	15	1
9	7	6	12
5	11	10	8
16	2	3	13

4	14	15	1
9	7	6	12
5	11	10	8
16	2	3	13

♃

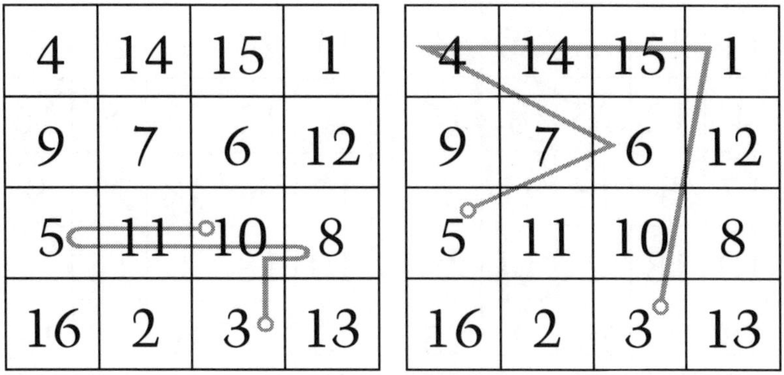

Jupiter

Jupiter 4x4	Sum along line 34	Total 136
IOPHIEL		HISMAEL
יהפיאל		הסמאל

30		
1		30
10		1
80		40
5		60
<u>10</u>		<u>5</u>
136		136

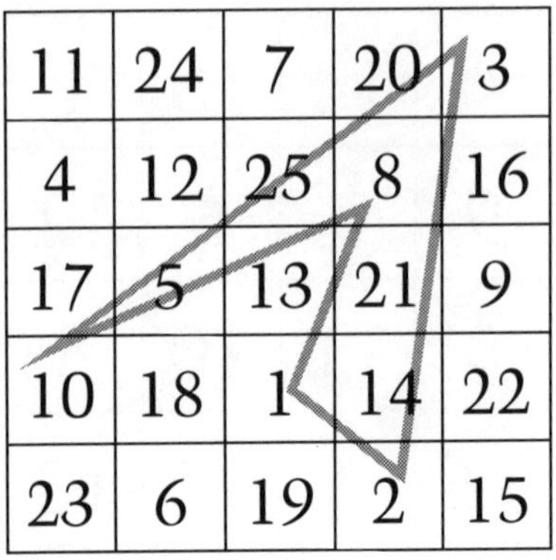
11 24 7 20 3
4 12 25 8 16
17 5 13 21 9
10 18 1 14 22
23 6 19 2 15

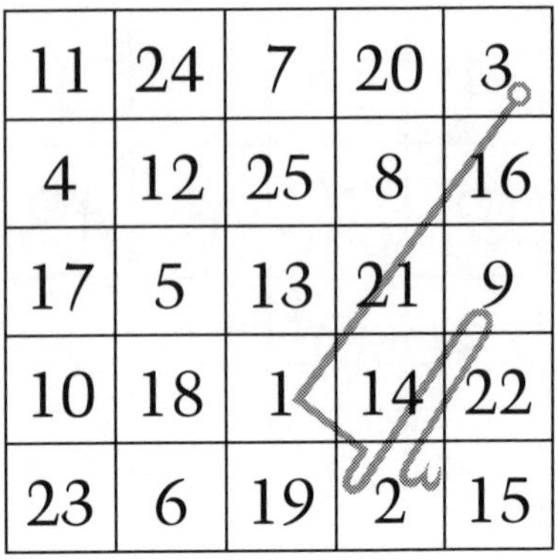
11 24 7 20 3
4 12 25 8 16
17 5 13 21 9
10 18 1 14 22
23 6 19 2 15

♂

Mars

Mars 5x5 **Sum along line 65** **Total 325**

GRAPHIEL
גראפיאל

30
1
10
80
1
200
3
325

BARZABEL
ברצאבאל

30
1
2
90
200
2
325

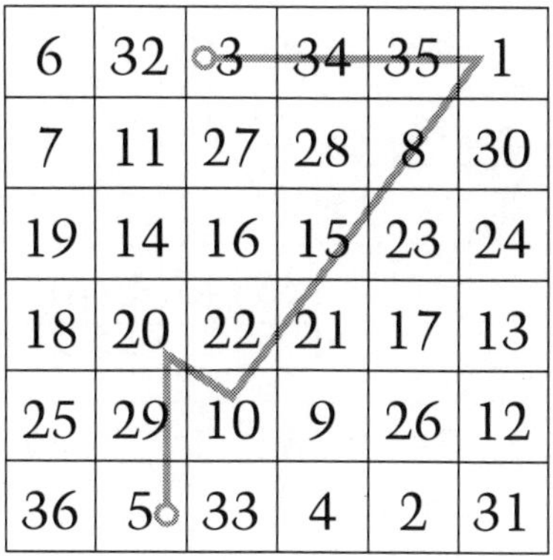

6 32 3 34 35 1
7 11 27 28 8 30
19 14 16 15 23 24
18 20 22 21 17 13
25 29 10 9 26 12
36 5 33 4 2 31

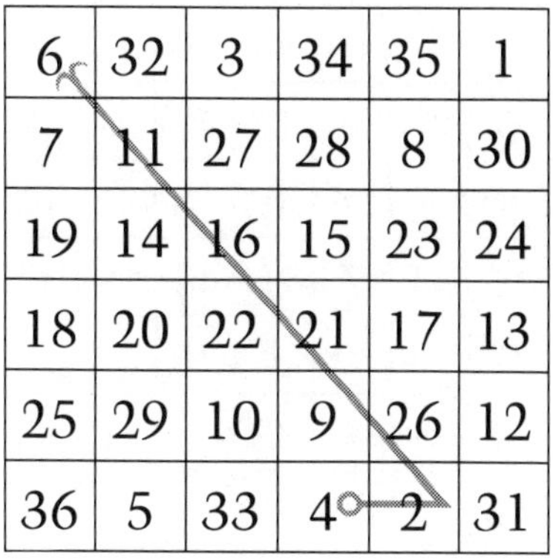

6 32 3 34 35 1
7 11 27 28 8 30
19 14 16 15 23 24
18 20 22 21 17 13
25 29 10 9 26 12
36 5 33 4 2 31

☉

Sun

Sun 6x6	**Sum along line 111**	**Total 666**
NACHIEL נכיאל		SORATH סורת
30 1 10 20 <u>50</u> 111		400 200 6 <u>60</u> 666

22	47	16	41	10	35	4
5	23	48	17	42	11	29
30	6	24	49	18	36	12
13	31	7	25	43	19	37
38	14	32	1	26	44	20
21	39	8	33	2	27	45
46	15	40	9	34	3	28

22	47	16	41	10	35	4
5	23	48	17	42	11	29
30	6	24	49	18	36	12
13	31	7	25	43	19	37
38	14	32	1	26	44	20
21	39	8	33	2	27	45
46	15	40	9	34	3	28

♀

Venus

Venus 7x7 **Sum along line 175** **Total 1225**

HAGIEL	KEDEMEL
הגיאל	קדמאל
30	30
1	1
10	40
3	4
5	100
49	175

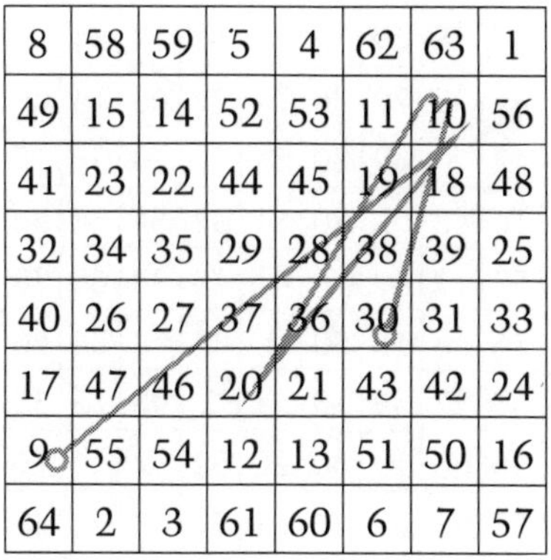

8	58	59	5	4	62	63	1
49	15	14	52	53	11	10	56
41	23	22	44	45	19	18	48
32	34	35	29	28	38	39	25
40	26	27	37	36	30	31	33
17	47	46	20	21	43	42	24
9	55	54	12	13	51	50	16
64	2	3	61	60	6	7	57

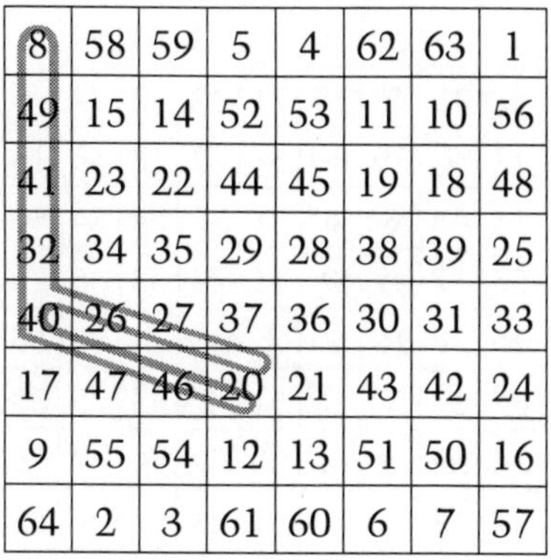

8	58	59	5	4	62	63	1
49	15	14	52	53	11	10	56
41	23	22	44	45	19	18	48
32	34	35	29	28	38	39	25
40	26	27	37	36	30	31	33
17	47	46	20	21	43	42	24
9	55	54	12	13	51	50	16
64	2	3	61	60	6	7	57

☿

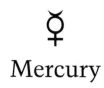

Mercury

Mercury 8x8 **Sum along line 260** **Total 2080**

TIRIEL טיריאל	TAPHTHARTHARATH תפתרתרת
	400
30	200
1	400
10	200
200	400
10	80
9	400
260	2080

37	78	29	70	21	62	13	54	5
6	38	79	30	71	22	63	14	46
47	7	39	80	31	72	23	55	15
16	48	8	40	81	32	64	24	56
57	17	49	9	41	73	33	65	25
26	58	18	50	1	42	74	34	66
67	27	59	10	51	2	43	75	35
36	68	19	60	20	52	3	44	76
77	28	69	20	61	21	53	4	45

37	78	29	70	21	62	13	54	5
6	38	79	30	71	22	63	14	46
47	7	39	80	31	72	23	55	15
16	48	8	40	81	32	64	24	56
57	17	49	9	41	73	33	65	25
26	58	18	50	1	42	74	34	66
67	27	59	10	51	2	43	75	35
36	68	19	60	20	52	3	44	76
77	28	69	20	61	21	53	4	45

☽

Moon

Moon 9x9 **Sum along line 369** **Total 3321**

HASMODAI
השמודאי

10
1
4
6
40
300
8
369

MALCHA
betharsitim
hed beruach
schehakim
שהקים
עד ברוח
בתרשיתים
מלכא

3321

18. The seals of the planets when imposed upon the magic squares, geometrically link the various numbers in the square into various groups. It has been shown that the magic square of n cells per side with its special arrangement of numbers, can be constructed from the regular array of numbers $1–n^2$ by a finite number of rotations and mirror reflections, and that these are recorded by the structure of the seal for that particular square. The interested reader is referred to an article by Karl Anton Nowotny, "The Construction of Certain Seals and Characters in the Work of Agrippa of Nettesheim," in the *Journal of the Warburg Institute*, vol. 12 (1949), pp. 46–57, in which a detailed analysis of this is given.

19. Although there is no text accompanying these two tables on the *Magical Calendar* plate, there is a description of the method of using these Horoscopic Tables in the *Magical Calendar* manuscript ascribed to Bacstrom in the Ferguson Collection:

> There follows an exact and at the same time careful explanation of the two tables of the Planets and the Celestial Signs. Alcander the philosopher composed these two tables. The first informs of the method of finding the ruling star of someones birth, and the other shows the horoscope of whatever birthdate one pleases, according as in the following explanation.
>
> **Explanation of the Alphabetic Tables of Alcander**
> Four letters are lacking in the Roman alphabet, which Alcander was able to make up from the alphabet itself, as evidently using the following "I," "V," "HI" and "HV" as consonants. Therefore in order for you to find the horoscope of someone's birthdate, take the numbers of the person's proper name, written in the nominative case, also the numbers of the names of their Father and Mother, of course also written in the nominative case, and divide the total sum by 12. The number remaining after this division represents the sign ascending in the hour of birth. If 1 it was Aries; if 2 - Taurus; 3 - Gemini; 4 - Cancer; 5 - Leo; 6 - Virgo; 7 - Libra; 8 - Scorpio; 9 - Saggitarius; 10 - Capricorn; 11 - Aquarius; 12 - Pisces.
>
> In order for you to discover the ruling planet of a person's birth,

proceed by the same method as above, with this difference—that the sum total of the person's name is divided by 9. And if the number remaining is 1 or 4, then it was the Sun; if 2 or 7, it was the Moon; 3 - Jupiter; 5 - Mercury; 6 - Venus; 8 - Saturn; 9 - Mars.

20. The Beatitudes are from the Sermon on the Mount; the most complete version appears in *Matthew* 5:3–10:

> Blessed are the poor in spirit: for theirs is the kingdom of heaven.
> Blessed are they that mourn: for they shall be comforted.
> Blessed are the meek: for they shall inherit the earth.
> Blessed are they that hunger and thirst after righteousness: for they shall be filled.
> Blessed are the merciful: for they shall obtain mercy.
> Blessed are the pure in heart: for they shall see God.
> Blessed are the peacemakers: for they shall be called the children of God.
> Blessed are they which are persecuted for righteousness' sake: For theirs is the kingdom of heaven.

21. As far as I have been able to ascertain, these symbols are unique to the *Magical Calendar*. They are depicted as if they were seal-tablets, the engraved plates of metal which would be pressed into wax to form an image.

They seem to form an integrated whole, with many cross connections and common elements between the different designs. All are characterized by a broad column running vertically, and most are right/left symmetrical about this center line. They have an odd quality and strength of form, which gives them a powerful presence.

The Seal of Solomon from this series can be found (in line drawn form) in many examples of the *Key of Solomon* manuscripts (Clavicula Salomonis), of which the facing illustration is only one example (Bibliothèque l'Arsenal MS. 2790):

Seal of Solomon from the *Key of Solomon*

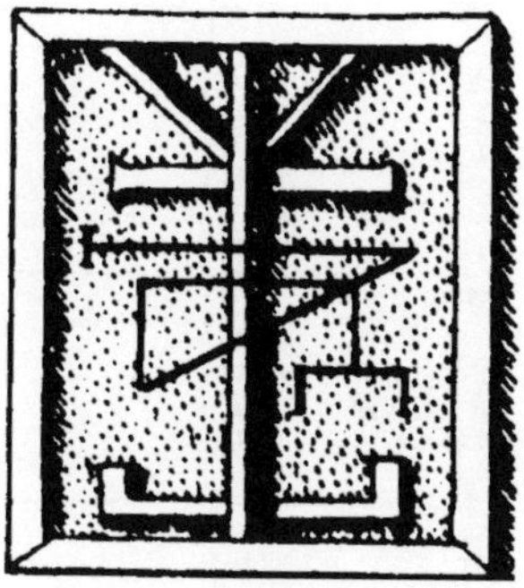

Seal of Solomon from the *Magical Calendar*

22. This table appears in the 1656 Robert Turner translation of Paracelsus *Of the Supreme Mysteries of Nature*, with the following text:

> An Election of Time to be observed in the transmutation of Metals—if at any time you shall desire to Transmute and change any Metal into another kind, as Gold into Silver, or rather Silver into Gold, it is necessary that you learn to elect a fit time for that purpose out of the Table following, whereby you shall easier, sooner, and without danger bring your work to your desired end.

To change into ☉.	☽ ♂ ♃ ♄ ☿	Begin when the Moon is in the sixth Degree of	♋ ♉ ♈ ♓ ♒ ♍	Always begin in the hour of that Planet whose Metal you would change.	☽ ♀ ♂ ♃ ♄ ☿
♄.	☉ ☽ ♂ ♀ ♃ ☿	Twenty Degrees of	♌ ♋ ♏ ♉ ♓ ♍		☉ ☽ ♂ ♀ ♃ ☿
☿.	☉ ☽ ♀ ♂ ♃ ♄	First Degree of	♌ ♋ ♉ ♏ ♓ ♒		☉ ☽ ♀ ♂ ♃ ♄
☽.	☉ ♀ ♂ ♃ ♄ ☿	In twelve Degrees of	♌ ♎ ♏ ♐ ♒ ♊		☉ ♀ ♂ ♃ ♄ ☿
♀.	☉ ☽ ♂ ♄ ♃ ☿	Ninth Degree of	♌ ♋ ♈ ♓ ♒ ♊	In the Hour of	☉ ☽ ♂ ♃ ♄ ☿
♂.	☉ ☾ ♀ ♃ ♄ ☿	Eighteenth Degree of	♌ ♋ ♉ ♐ ♑ ♍	The Hour of	☉ ☽ ♀ ♃ ♄ ☿
♃.	☉ ☽ ♀ ♂ ♄ ☿	The third Degree of	♌ ♋ ♎ ♏ ♒ ♍	Hour of	☉ ☽ ♀ ♂ ♄ ☿

> Take this one example only, and so work by the rest; as, if you would change Luna into Sol, begin when the Moon is in Six Degrees of Cancer, in the hour of the Moon, and so observe the rest, according to this table. For the observation of time is not to be held of a vain account in the transmutation of the Metals, for all negotiations and actions in this world are most happily brought to perfection, which are begun with due respect to the course and influences of the Celestial Bodies; for our mortal bodies are ruled according to the operations of the Superior Bodies of the Firmament, and they are ordained for that purpose by Almighty God the Creator, and do bring unto us, both health, sickness, infirmities, and health again: and in like manner the times are to be noted, and duly observed in Medical Operations, that their virtues may work the more powerful effects.

23. The two Sacrosanct Pentacles of the Nine Angelic Choirs are both outwardly triangular in form, and have their three sides corresponding to the three Choirs of Angels that constitute the third or lowest hierarchy, the Principalities, Archangels and Angels. The first pentacle refers to the fact that the Angels are stationed in the little world, with responsibility for the evolution of individual human beings; the Principalities are in charge of the evolution of states, nations and races; while the Archangels mediate between these two diverse realms.

In the center of the first pentacle we find a hexagon and two of the first hierarchy, the Seraphim and Cherubim, inscribed together with a hexagram which has "ADONAI" within its vertices, and the Tetragrammaton lying at its centre. Mediating between the outer triangle and the central hexagon, are the Hebrew letters ydç Shaddai, the Almighty.

The center of the second pentacle also has a hexagram, but within this is inscribed a triangle containing the Tetragrammaton acrostic:

י

י ה

י ה ו

י ה ו ה

This gives us the Ten, the true esoteric number of the hierarchies, i.e. the nine Choirs of Angels plus Man, the tenth hierarchy. Mediating between this inner symbol and the outer triangle are the Hebrew letters ישו (Jesu).

24. In classical mythology the Muses were the nine daughters of Jupiter and Mnemosyne. They have the following associations:

	Usual Attributes	**Depicted with**	**Esoteric**
Calliope	Epic poetry	wax tablet and pencil	Science of Man
Euterpe	Lyric poetry	Double flute	Medicine, Magic
Erato	Erotic poetry and mime	Small lyre	Science of the Elements
Melpomene	Tragedy	Tragic mask and ivy leaf	Science of life and death, rebirth
Thalia	Comedy	Comic mask and ivy leaf	Science of stones, plants, and animals
Polyhymnia	Sacred Hymns	Veiled in an attitude of thought	Science of souls in the other life; Divination
Terpsichore	Choral song and dance	Lyre	Terrestrial physics
Clio	History	A scroll	Psychology
Urania	Astronomy	A celestial globe	Astrology

25. These Bacchic Muses are rather obscure and I have not been able to find further details of them all:

Bassarius	- a title of Bacchus, from the wolf skins worn by the devotees.
Lysius	- either from "lyssa" meaning madness or frenzy, or from "Lycaeus," a lofty mountain in Arcadia where Pan was worshipped.
Silenus	- a satyr who brought up and instructed Bacchus. He possessed prophetic powers, which he could be made to exercise by surrounding him with chains of flowers.
Lyaeus	- "the one who sets free," wine.

26. These ten pairs of seals give, in a pictorial form, a knowledge of the ten Sephiroth and their correspondences with the planets, the archangels, the names of God, the angelic hosts, and the hierarchies. I have included in brackets those correspondences that have been in one or two cases omitted.

Primum Mobile Assigned to God the Father Hexagram
God is the simplicity of divinity
(Seraphim) Eheieh אהיה (Chaioth ha Qadesh)
Metatron, the prince of the death-bringers
Kether כתר Metatron

Heaven of the stars First Cause The Creator Pentagram
Wisdom, the first-born of God
Cherubim Jah י (Auphanim)
The Cherubim, the form or wheel of archetypes
(Chokmah) חכמה (Ratziel)

Saturn Octagon
The Holy Spirit of the Divine Majesty
Thrones Jehovah Elohim יהוה אלהים Aralim
Kindle in me the fire of Love and Charity
Binah בינה Zaphkiel

Jupiter Triangle
The scepter in his right hand; in Heaven there is mercy
Dominations El אל (Chasmalim)
Whose mercy does not end; God is enduring and merciful
Chesed חסד Zadkiel

Mars Octagon
God our King; the king of glory before the ages
Powers Elohim Gibor אלהים גבור Seraphim
The great King above all; the God of Glory
Geburah גבורה Camael

Sun Circle
Hod and beauty in his sight
Virtues Eloah אלוה Malachim
Tiphereth and strength in his sight
Tiphereth תפארת Raphael

Venus Heptagon
The conqueror in Israel does not spare . . .
Principalities Jehovah Sabaoth יהוה צבאות (Elohim)
. . . punishment, nor is it a man who acts
Netzach נצח Haniel

Mercury Pentagon
You have put on beauty, clad with light
Archangels Elohim Sabaoth אלהים צבאות (Bene Elohim)
Give me the wisdom which is yours
Hod הוד Michael

Moon Vesica
God giving increase to all
Angels Shaddai שדי Cherubim
Rule your body and mind with your spirit
Iesod יסוד Gabriel

Soul of the World			Square
Your reign is an everlasting reign			
(Man)	Adonai אדני	Ishim	
Give prophetic wisdom			
Malkuth מאלכות	Sandalophon	World-Soul	

27. The twelve lettered name of God has here been garbled, but it is not too difficult to see what was intended.

Father	אב
Son	בן and ו
Holy Spirit	רוח הקדש

28. These Angels of the twelve Signs are also found in the *Sworn Book of Honourius*. I have not been able to locate a source for their sigils.

29. These magic squares associated with the twelve Signs are rather perplexing. Two are not squares at all but rather 4x3 rectangles; there are four 4x4 squares and six 3x3 squares in all. At first sight one would reckon they are fragments of some larger magic square, however, I have only been able to positively identify two of them as such:

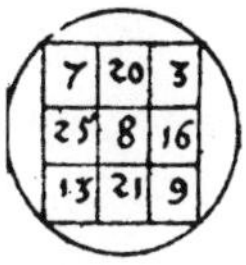

♈ is the top right hand corner of the Mars square.

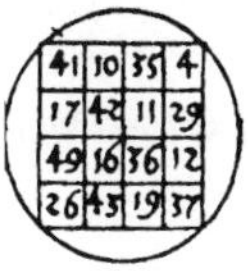

♉ is the top right hand corner of the Venus square.

30. The source for the pairs of seals connected with the twelve Signs is Paracelsus *Of the Supreme Mysteries of Nature,* also known as the *Archidoxes of Magic,* which was translated into English by Robert Turner in 1656.

31. In Robert Fludd's system of medicine outlined in his *Medica Catholica* (1629), we find the "fortress of health" of the individual under siege from the four quarters by spiritual beings and their hosts of lesser entities, bringing various diseases. The sound man is able to fight off these influences through the aid of the four Archangels.

Quarter	Spiritual being bringing illness	Lesser hosts mediating illness	Influence countered by
East	Oriens	Samael	Michael
South	Amayon	Azazel	Uriel
West	Paymon	Azael	Raphael
North	Egyn	Mahazel	Gabriel

Of these four archetypal beings bringing ill health, three would seem to be equivalent to the four Principal Spirits in the *Magical Calendar* list; however, the correspondences do not work out in detail.

32. This straightforward ephemeris of the Sun gives its sign and degree for each day of the year.

33. The ornaments or vestments of the Priesthood of the Jews, are described in *Exodus* chapters 28 and 29.

Ordinary priests wear four white linen vestments when ministering in the Temple.

Foemoralia	breeches
Tunica	tunic
Cingulus	girdle
Cap	instead of the Tiara of the High Priest

The High Priest wore four additional vestments:

Stolatalar	blue sleeveless robe with bells at the hem
Superhumer	the Ephod, worn over the robe and made of gold, blue, purple and scarlet fine linen
Rationale	breastplate containing the oracular Urim and Thummim and twelve precious stones set in four rows with the names of the tribes of Israel engraved thereon.
Gold Plate	engraved with the phrase 'Holy to the Lord' worn on the forehead with the mitre.

34. **Universal dial, comprising the equal magical Bohemian and Italian hours.**
The determination of the planetary rulership of the hours, essential to the Western magical tradition, was based on a division of the day and night into twelve equal "hours" each. Thus in summer, a daytime "hour" was much longer than a nighttime one, and in winter, the reverse. This is a design for a sundial which would indicate the daytime hours according to each month of the year (shown by the signs of the Zodiac).

35. The lowest compartment of the *Calendar* reads:

> These are the things which we have gathered into this our calendar, in a varied compilation made with great labor and research, for an introduction to natural magic. If the viewers will scrutinize with great care the things that are written here, they will be able to follow a complete doctrine of the magical art, as well as infallible experiments. But as for you, malevolent slanderers of low and insipid ignorance, sons of iniquity, flee from these things of ours and leave them untouched. For to criticize is easy, but to emulate is hard; and in great matters it is difficult to please many, while to please everyone is nigh impossible.

Magnum Opus Hermetic Sourceworks

The Magical Calendar
The Mosaical Philosophy—Cabala
The Crowning of Nature
The Rosicrucian Emblems of Cramer
The Hermetic Garden of Daniel Stolcius
The Rosary of the Philosophers
The Amphitheatre Engravings of Heinrich Khunrath
Splendor Solis
The 'Key' of Jacob Boehme
The Revelation of Revelations of Jane Leade
A Commentary on the Mutus Liber
The Steganographia of Trithemius
The Origin and Structure of the Cosmos
Goethe's Fairy Tale of the Green Snake and the Beautiful Lily
A Treatise on Angel Magic
The Paradoxical Emblems of Freher
The Heptarchia Mystica of John Dee
Commentary on the Chymical Wedding
Alchemical Engravings of Mylius
The Five Books of Mystical Exercises of John Dee
Atalanta Fugiens of Michael Maier
The Kabbalistic Diagrams of Rosenroth

In addition to issuing the Magnum Opus Hermetic Sourceworks series, PHANES PRESS publishes many fine books which relate to the philosophical and spiritual traditions of the Western world. To obtain a copy of our current catalogue, please write:

PHANES PRESS
PO BOX 6114
GRAND RAPIDS, MI 49516
USA

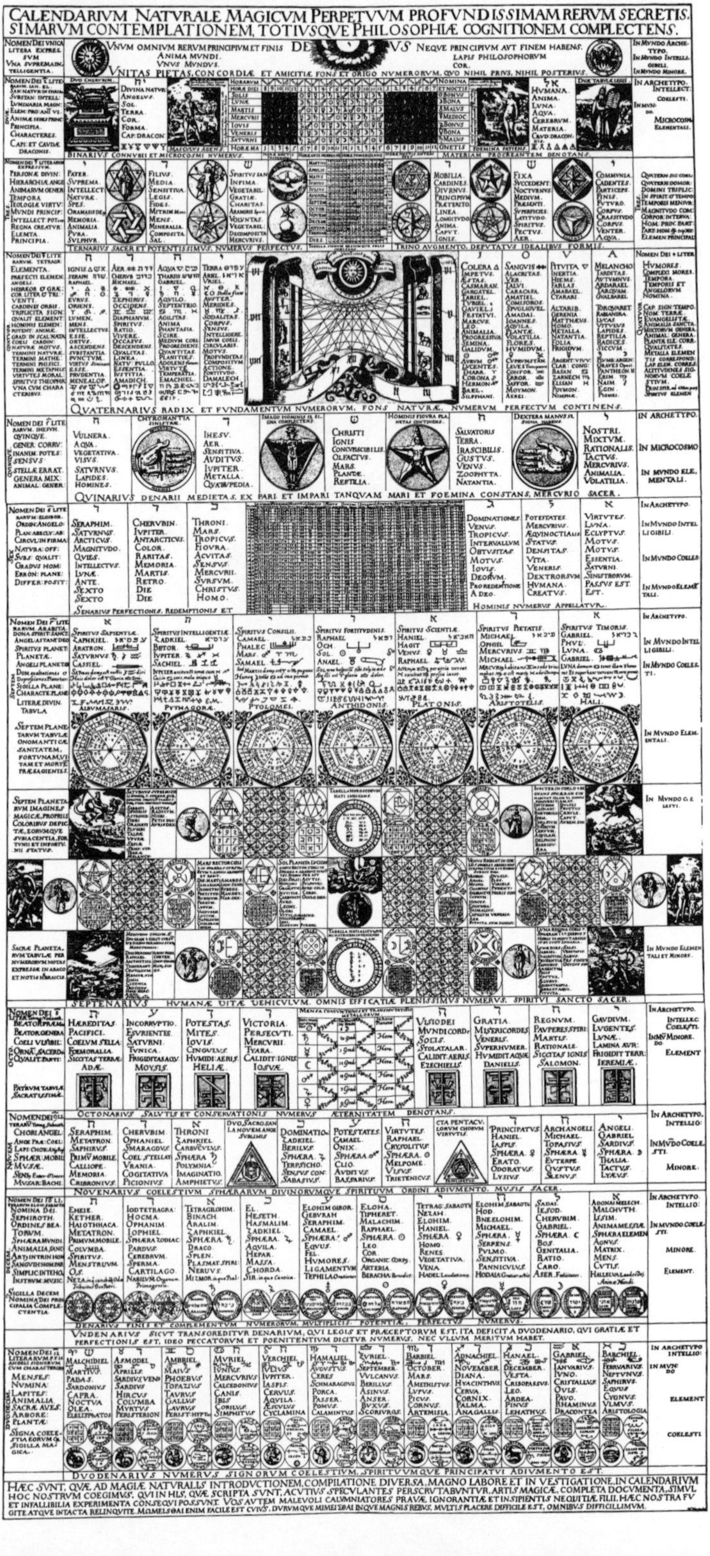

CALENDARIVM NATVRALE MAGICVM PERPETVVM PROFVNDISSIMAM RERVM SECRETISSIMARVM CONTEMPLATIONEM, TOTIVSQVE PHILOSOPHIÆ COGNITIONEM COMPLECTENS.
VNVM OMNIVM RERVM PRINCIPIVM ET FINIS DEVS NEQVE PRINCIPIVM AVT FINEM HABENS.
ANIMA MVNDI. VNVS MVNDVS. LAPIS PHILOSOPHORVM COR.
VNITAS PIETAS, CONCORDIÆ ET AMICITIÆ FONS ET ORIGO NVMERORVM, QVO NIHIL PRIVS, NIHIL POSTERIVS.
BINARIVS CONNVBII ET MICROCOSMI NVMERVS. MATERIAM PROCREANTEM DENOTANS.
TERNARIVS SACER ET POTENTISSIMVS, NVMERVS PERFECTVS. TRINO AVGMENTO, DEPVTATVS IDEALIBVS FORMIS.
QVATERNARIVS RADIX ET FVNDAMENTVM NVMERORVM, FONS NATVRÆ, NVMERVM PERFECTVM CONTINENS.
QVINARIVS DENARII MEDIETAS, EX PARI ET IMPARI TANQVAM MARI ET FOEMINA CONSTANS, MERCVRIO SACER.
SENARIVS PERFECTIONIS, REDEMPTIONIS ET HOMINIS NVMERVS APPELLATVR.
SEPTENARIVS HVMANÆ VITÆ VEHICVLVM, OMNIS EFFICATIÆ PLENISSIMVS NVMERVS, SPIRITVI SANCTO SACER.
OCTONARIVS SALVTIS ET CONSERVATIONIS NVMERVS ÆTERNITATEM DENOTANS.
NOVENARIVS COELESTIVM SPHÆRARVM DIVINORVMQVE SPIRITVVM ORDINI ADIVMENTO. MVSIS SACER.
DENARIVS FINIS ET COMPLEMENTVM NVMERORVM, MVLTIPLICIS POTENTIÆ, PERFECTVS NVMERVS.
VNDENARIVS SICVT TRANSGREDITVR DENARIVM, QVI LEGIS ET PRÆCEPTORVM EST, ITA DEFICIT A DVODENARIO, QVI GRATIÆ ET PERFECTIONIS EST, IDEO PECCATORVM ET POENITENTIVM DICITVR NVMERVS, NEC VLLVM MERITVM HABET.
DVODENARIVS NVMERVS SIGNORVM COELESTIVM, SPIRITVVMQVE PRINCIPATVI ADIVMENTO EST.
HÆC SVNT, QVÆ AD MAGIÆ NATVRALIS INTRODVCTIONEM, COMPILATIONE DIVERSA, MAGNO LABORE ET IN VESTIGATIONE, IN CALENDARIVM HOC NOSTRVM COEGIMVS, QVI IN HIS, QVÆ SCRIPTA SVNT, ACVTIVS SPECVLANTES PERSCRVTABVNTVR, ARTIS MAGICÆ, COMPLETA DOCVMENTA, SIMVL ET INFALLIBILIA EXPERIMENTA CONSEQVI POSSVNT. VOS AVTEM MALEVOLI CALVMNIATORES PRAVÆ IGNORANTIÆ ET INSIPIENTIS NEQVITIÆ FILII, HÆC NOSTRA FVGITE ATQVE INTACTA RELINQVITE. MΩMEISΘAI ENIM FACILE EST CVIVS, DVRVMQVE MIMEIΣΘAI INQVE MAGNIS REBVS, MVLTIS PLACERE DIFFICILE EST, OMNIBVS DIFFICILLIMVM.

The Magical Calendar Limited Edition Print

Issued in conjunction with this publication of *The Magical Calendar* is an 18 x 36 inch, poster size, high quality reproduction of the original Magical Calendar which is suitable for framing.

To obtain a copy of this print anywhere in the world, send a check or money order for $12.00 in U.S. funds made payable to Phanes Press. Mail to:

MAGICAL CALENDAR PRINT
PHANES PRESS
PO BOX 6114
GRAND RAPIDS, MI 49516
USA